# ULTIMATE
# LIFE LESSONS

## TAKE CONTROL OF YOUR LIFE ...
## INSTEAD OF LETTING LIFE CONTROL YOU

*The ultimate life guide packed with proven real-life experiences of how experts have taken their lives to success.*

EVE GRACE-KELLY    VINDEN GRACE    TRACY REPCHUK

**Ultimate Life Lessons**

First published in 2010 by

Ecademy Press
48 St Vincent Drive, St Albans, Hertfordshire, AL1 5SJ

info@ecademy-press.com www.ecademy-press.com

Printed and Bound by Lightning Source in the UK and USA

Set by Charlotte Mouncey

Printed on acid-free paper from managed forests.
This book is printed on demand, so no copies will be
remaindered or pulped.

ISBN 978-1-905823-92-5

In purchasing this book, you are entitled to $000's worth of free bonuses from co-authors of this book.

Visit

**www.UltimateLifeLessons.com**

to claim them and insert the following number where indicated

**EVT201011A**

# Acclaim For Ultimate Life Lessons

*"Read this book and change your life"*

Erin Pizzey, international founder of the first shelter for victims of domestic violence in the world and best-selling novelist

*"Ultimate Life Lessons is a great compilation of wisdom to support readers to live their most empowered, fulfilled, abundant and optimum lives. Study each lesson, map it on to your life, and watch your life transform to meet your wildest expectations."*

Dr. Joe Rubino

CEO, www.CenterForPersonalReinvention.com

Creator, www.TheSelfEsteemBook.com and www.SuccessCodeSystem.com

*"A wonderful way to learn some important lessons in life, while enjoying your own personal growth!"*

Ryan Higgins

Creator of Mind Movies, www.MindMovies.com

*"The Ultimate Life Lesson seems to be that school is always in session – this book will help you make the grade"*

Julie Starr, author of The Coaching Manual and Brilliant Coaching

*"Our lives are based on an accumulation of bits of knowledge that moved us in some way towards how we show up in the world each day. Ultimate Life Lessons is like having access to a myriad of bits of knowledge in one big volume to drink in and absorb as we're ready. Page after page of wisdom and best of all, activities to put that wisdom to use in your own life. Wise, useful and fun to read. Don't try to live life without it!"*

Elisabeth Donati

The Financial Literacy Lady

www.CampMillionaire.com

*"This book may well be a fantastic catalyst for many people to be inspired to change direction, obtain greater fulfillment and achieve more of what they want. Great job!"*

John Seeley M.A.

Life Coach

www.GetUnstuck.com

www.GetUnstuckForKids.com

*"A superb mix of life lessons from coaches, entrepreneurs and other successful teachers. I love the bite-sized approach to each topic and chapter. So many 'AH-HA' moments throughout that I will revisit over and over. I'm proud to endorse Ultimate Life Lessons...just terrific!"*

Jimmy Sweeney, President, www.honesteonline.com

*"Seek out that particular mental attribute which makes you feel most deeply and vitally alive, along with which comes the inner voice which says, 'This is the real me,' and when you have found that attitude, follow it."*
William James

# Acknowledgements

## *Thank you to everyone*

In putting together a multi-author book like this, or indeed any book, there are so many direct and indirect contributors. Eve and Vinden would like to offer a heartfelt thank you to all of our co-authors, many of whom have become great friends. Without their contributions, this book wouldn't have the same variety. All of our highly successful contributors have something worthwhile to say and all of them give back to society in numerous ways.

We want to thank all of our mentors along the way:

- Tracy Repchuk, our lead Joint Venture partner in this project. Her internet wisdom has been invaluable.

- Jonathan Jay, our business mentor. He, Fiona Challis and Paul Green have worked with us at The National Association of Business Owners, to focus us on gettng this project into great shape.

- Rich Schefren, for his sound business coaching, based on proven, offline business and marketing techniques.

Other people who have been really kind and helpful include:

- Mindy Gibbins-Klein for her unstinting support and wise guidance via her broad book-writing coaching knowledge in how to write this book and publishing via her company, Ecademy Press.

- Bev James of the Entrepreneurs' Business Academy for her kindness in introducing us to several superb co-authors for the book.

- Stephanie J Hale for her sound counsel regarding this book project from her own extensive book-writing and coaching experience.

- Dianna Bonner for the great photos of Eve and Vinden. Dianna has the ability to put her clients at ease always bringing out the best in people, whatever the occasion or event. To see some of her work visit www.WorldVisionPhotos.co.uk or email her on info@WorldVisionPhotos.co.uk.

To all of our clients, we'd like to say a big thank you for your feedback, sharing your success stories with us and for letting us share in your journey!

To all of our Joint Venture partners in this book, thank you so much for your highly valued contributions and we're really excited to be working with you on the various business enterprises launching as a result of working together on this book project. It's amazing what can come out of an idea for a book....

Gratitude also goes to our families and dear friends for their patience during the last few months where our heads have been down, working hard on this book and the associated projects. Thank you for your forbearance with our low profiles during this time!

## *who made it all possible*

## *BE More – DO More – ACHIEVE More*™

Quantum Coaching and Consulting Group Limited (QCC Group)

14 Hanover Street (3rd Floor)

Hanover Square

Mayfair

London

W1S 1YH

United Kingdom

enquiries@QCCGroup.com

*"Don't GO through life, GROW through life."*
Eric Butterworth

# Preface

We've always been interested in self-improvement, personal development and growth. It means being open to new ideas; learning from the wisdom of those who have already gained the experience; not assuming that yours is the only answer. On our journey through life, we've been to a myriad of seminars, taken loads of courses, read stacks of self-help books.... Have they helped? You bet they have! Why? Because we're open-minded: we know that we don't have all of the answers to life's challenges.

What we've assembled here is the combined wisdom of over 30 superbly talented co-authors.

The life lessons from all of the contributors are in their own words, expressing their own thoughts and feelings.

## Who will you learn from?

- **Eve Grace-Kelly**: "One of the UK's leading Success Coaches" (Jonathan Jay), a true outside the box thinker and co-author of 5 other books. Co-founder and CEO of a coaching, consulting, training and wellness company, QCCgroup.com.

- **Vinden Grace**: A leading Digital Coach, teaching people Worldwide how to be successful in Internet-based business. Co-author of 5 other books. Co-founder of a coaching, consulting, training and wellness company, QCCgroup.com.

- **Tracy Repchuk**: #1 Woman Speaker in the World for Internet Marketing. Bestselling author of 31 Days to Millionaire Marketing Miracles, International speaker and motivator and award-winning entrepreneur of over 25 years.

- **Jonathan Jay:** He founded the UK's largest Life and Business Coach training school, The Coaching Academy, which he later sold for millions! He has now set up and is Chairman of SuccessTrack and the National Association of Business Owners. He's author of three books and star of TV's 'Now I'm The Boss', and the UK's highest-paid business consultant.

- Several of the TV stars of the UK's C4 and America's FOX network series *Secret Millionaire*.

  - **Gill Fielding:** An international public speaker, writer and a presenter on e.g. the BBC, ITV, and CNBC. A self-made millionaire who has been also featured on BBC's *The Apprentice* series. She acts as a UK Government adviser and as a mentor in James Caan's (of BBC TV's *Dragons' Den* fame) and Bev James' Entrepreneurs' Business Academy.

  - **Emma Harrison**, who also starred in a TV program recently about getting jobs for people and who founded and runs A4e, a company in that field generating income of over £145 million.

  - **Kevin Green:** Wales's most successful residential landlord, a self-made millionaire with a property portfolio of £29 million. Kevin runs a property investment training business.

  - **Seema Sharma:** Multiple award winner, CEO of Smile Impressions Dental Practices, and founder of Medibyte and Dentabyte – medical and dental management and training consultancies. Better known to many as Channel 4's 'Slumdog Secret Millionaire'!

  - **Caroline Marsh:** A highly successful buy-to-let property investor with a personal and business development coaching business.

  - **Gurbaksh Chahal:** An award-wining entrepreneur, he sold his Internet advertising company to Yahoo! He's also appeared on The Oprah Winfrey Show.

- **Penny Power:** Social Networking Expert, Author, Entrepreneur and founder of Ecademy.com, with over half a million subscribers in her world-wide network of 200+ countries. She is a mentor in James Caan's (of BBC TV's *Dragons' Den* fame) and Bev James' Entrepreneurs' Business Academy.

- **Dr William Davey:** Former Physician to Her Majesty Queen Elizabeth II. Cutting-edge researcher and innovator in diet and lifestyle, leading his clients to longer and healthier lives.

- **Bev James:** MD of the UK's largest Life and Business Coach training school, The Coaching Academy and co-founder of the Entrepreneurs' Business Academy with James Caan of the BBC series *Dragons' Den*.

- **Stephanie J Hale:** A publishing expert and writing coach, helping authors to write, promote and pitch their books.

- **Susanne Jorgensen:** A psychologist, coach, author and a leading Dating Coach.

- **Katie Moore:** Entrepreneur and investor who built an online community of 70,000 entrepreneurs.

- **Kelly Morrisey:** One of America's leading Divorce Coaches, dealing internationally with recovering from divorce and personal growth strategies.

- **Mindy Gibbins-Klein:** An international speaker and author, who is founder and director of REAL Thought Leaders, The Book Midwife® and Ecademy Press business publishing.

- **Curly Martin:** An international speaker, a pioneer of life coaching in Europe and the founder of a very successful coach training company.

- **Peter Thomson:** One of the UK's leading strategists on business and personal growth.

- **Marie O'Riordan:** Worked on radio and TV (e.g. CNN journalist) and award-winning short film-maker. She has interviewed many Hollywood stars and was the last person to interview Mother Theresa.

- **Debbie Allen:** One of the world's leading authorities on innovative marketing and the author of five books.

- **Kathleen Ronald:** Expert on Business Networking and Follow-up, Speaker/Trainer, Business Consultant, and founder of Speaktacular!

- **Janet Beckers:** Founder of a successful and dynamic online community; an international speaker, best-selling author and mentor. Recently voted Australian Marketer of The Year.

- **Andy Harrington:** One of the world's premier authorities on the psychology of peak performance, personal achievement and the art of influence.

- **John Lees:** One of the UK's best-known career strategists. He regularly tops the list with the best-selling careers book by a British author.

- **Glenn Harrold:** The UK's best selling self-help audio author, who has recovered from serious drug and alcohol abuse.

- **John Purkiss:** A leading head-hunter, he recruits senior executives and board members for a wide range of companies.

- **Nick James:** Internationally acclaimed Internet marketing guru, business coach and speaker.

- **Amanda van der Gulik:** A homeschooling mom-preneur, passionate about empowering kids with life-skills, self-esteem building skills, and teaching children and teens about money.

- **Paul Avins:** Author of *Business SOS* and founder of The Business Wealth Club Franchise whose track record includes generating over £100 million in new sales and profits for the businesses he's coached.

- **Toby Garbett:** An Olympian and two-time World Champion rower. A fitness consultant and Pilates instructor, providing training to corporate and private clients.

- **Emma Tiebens:** She teaches entrepreneurs how to create a powerful online presence for their business using technology to build and foster business relationships with people.

- **Dr Jane Lewis:** Coach, consultant and trainer. She offers tailored career coaching programs to women who have hit the glass ceiling at work.

- **Dr Joe Kasper:** Master level health coach, an exercise therapist and speaker.

## What can Life Lessons teach you?

There is a saying: "You are what you eat," meaning that if you feed your body with good quality foods and in the right quantities, you will be healthy and suffer less illness as a result. Well, the same goes for ensuring we have a healthy mind and a healthy and fulfilling experience in life.

But, just as it can be tempting to reach out for the easiest food option when we're busy or tired, we sometimes take the easiest option in our life decisions. We know it's not the best decision but for some reason, whether it's due to elements such as confidence, self-esteem, or beliefs, we make decisions that are not necessarily in our best interest. It could be taking the path of least resistance. Often, though, it's as a result of a lack of understanding an action's implications, or of taking the time to assess what things have gone wrong in the past, and what we can do to improve our future decisions.

Life lessons are the values and views that you acquire over the course of your lifetime based on events in your life. And, within this book, we have a combined set of life experiences, and hence life lessons, of a staggering 1,450 years (give or take a year or two)! Everyone within this book is passionate about helping you to positively impact the way you experience life; to help you get the most out of your relationships with people; achieve the careers you want; make your business a great success and generally help you to attain your goals in life, whether in your personal life or related to your career or business.

We all want to share some of our passion with you through sharing some of our life lessons – our pains, our successes, and our learning from both of these.

With all of the co-authors' combined experiences of life, you would think that, when we are faced with difficult circumstances, there are always lessons that come with them that we could pick up. However, we often don't discern the lessons because our focus is not on the lessons, but on the circumstances or the event itself. When you make a decision to focus on the lesson that comes with the situation, you may well find a desire deep within you to want to go back and change certain things to prevent the event from happening again. You can't: all you can do is learn from the lesson and be mindful of it in future. Why? Well, as Albert Einstein is reputed to have said: "[The definition of] insanity is doing the same thing over and over again but expecting different results." In other words, we must learn from life if we are to improve our lives.

The sad thing is that we may face certain adversities over and over because we don't learn the lesson that we were intended to learn. Sometimes the difficulties may be different but the lesson is generally the same.

We all experience lessons in life every single day of our existence. Some teaching we notice, some we don't, but ultimately, our life lessons help us to prepare for and make better, more informed decisions, the next time we encounter a similar situation.

You have to make a positive choice to take life's lessons, adapt them, run with them, and apply them to your daily existence in order to get more of what you want from life.

Have you faced a problem or situation many times over? Was it due to a lack on your part of learning lessons? Life lessons are hands-on. They provide experience and wisdom. We just need to become more self-aware in order to understand and use them.

We've certainly learned a lot of lessons in putting this book together. Eve is forever the optimist and very much a front-loaded task person in that she wants everyone to do everything now! When we, Eve, Vinden and Tracy, first joined forces on our journey in pulling this project together, we thought we'd have it all sewn up within four months. But it's taken a bit longer than that..... well, twice as long, actually! But we think the wait has been worth it. During the process, we have worked with some fabulous, inspiring people, and are really pleased that they also share our passion for enhancing the quality of people's lives.

We hope you get a lot of value out of this book – our combined learning – and that the exercises will help you get more out of both our life's lessons and your own.

Share your life lesson with other readers on - www.UltimateLifeLessonsClub.com and add to the 1,450 years' worth of life experiences that went into this book. We may feature your lesson in a future book in this series!

To your continued success in life.

Warmest wishes,

Eve Grace-Kelly        Vinden Grace        Tracy Repchuk

*"There is one subject you don't study in school, but it is the most crucial subject that has the greatest impact on your own happiness and quality of life. That subject is YOU!*

*The journey inside of you is the most exciting adventure you will ever embark on. By discovering the amazing person that you are, you will be better able to understand others. You will find meaning in your life, make great choices in your careers and lifestyles, and create your own happiness."*

Eve Grace-Kelly

# Foreword

**Jonathan Jay**

**Chairman NABO & SuccessTrack**

Just as alchemists once searched for the secret formula that would turn lead into gold, business owners today scour books, attend workshops and quiz others to discover the elusive secret of success.

Some believe that if they work harder and longer, wealth and happiness will immediately follow. Some think that if they attend one more course, they'll finally have all they need to make money and achieve their goals. Others are convinced that if they hire more staff and rent bigger premises, success will miraculously arrive.

I know this because I once believed success was inevitable if I worked (ridiculously) long hours, rented impressive office space and hired more and more staff. I was wrong but it took one business failure for the realization to begin to sink in.

Eventually, by the time I was down to my last £145, had mountains of debt, my house was about to be repossessed and my telephone had been cut off, I began to see that my 'recipe for success' was hopelessly flawed.

My most vivid memory of that time is sitting in my bedroom, looking at yet another reminder letter from my bank manager, and crying. Where have I gone wrong? I didn't have a clue.

I was so hungry for success and wanted to be the owner of a thriving business, but it was clear that my way wasn't going to work. At that point, I made one of the best decisions of my life: I looked for someone who was already successful and listened to his advice.

I chose to follow the advice of Brian Tracy, one of the world's most successful business and sales coaches – another great life-changing decision! I couldn't actually afford Brian's personal mentoring fees but I listened to his audio program to the point I nearly wore it out.

Around that time, I became aware that more and more people were talking about 'life coaching', the American motivational technique. I realized that no one in the UK was providing coach training and yet there was an obvious demand. Soon afterwards, I decided to take a big risk – I used my life savings – that £145 – to hold the UK's first coach training event. The response was great – 27 people attended.

My bank manager sent me a letter the following week, querying the fact, that in the time he'd been away on holiday, I'd cleared my overdraft and was actually in profit for the first time in years. He thought there'd been some sort of clerical error. No, I was happy to tell him, I've hit upon another secret of success – give people what they really want.

Bolstered by my initial success, I put on another coach training event and another. By the 20th event, I was a millionaire! And although I didn't realize it at the time, I had started the coaching revolution in the UK.

My business became known as The Coaching Academy and for the eight years I ran it (I sold it for millions of pounds in 2007), we trained over 16,000 people from 52 countries in business and life coaching. Our courses launched the careers of the majority of professional coaches in the UK, many of whom have gone on to become authors and TV celebrities.

Of course, I'd like to tell you that everything I did was perfect but that wouldn't be true. I made some major mistakes during the eight years I was Chairman of The Coaching Academy – I spent the first six years of the business working 12-hour days, seven days a week and began to burn out. I experienced cash-flow problems, staffing problems, marketing problems, delegation problems. At times, I struggled to find new clients and customers... then I discovered a better, easier and more successful way of doing business.

With what I discovered, I was able to slash my 60-80 hour working week down to one seven-hour day...to reduce my staff from 27 to seven ... cut my sales team from six down to one AND DOUBLE MY TURNOVER AND QUADRUPLE MY PROFIT!

I learnt what every highly successful person (and chef) knows... that simplicity is best. It's so easy to make running a business (or your life, for that matter) really complicated but it doesn't have to be like that.

So I stopped micro-managing the business and that's when the business really boomed. In the words of the world's leading business expert, Michael Gerber, I no longer 'worked in' but 'worked on' my business. Suddenly, I had the freedom I wanted – I had a lot more time on my hands, I could take holidays whenever I chose and I could finally achieve that mystical state of 'life-work' balance that I'd read so much about.

I discovered another great success secret... if you make a mistake, learn from it and move on really fast. Don't spend hours agonizing over what might have been or worse, ignoring it and hoping it will disappear. It never does.

Trying to do everything myself was one of my biggest mistakes but it's something I no longer do. Now, I hire in experts – I only have a handful of full-time staff and the rest of my business is carried out by freelance experts. Yes, I'm sure if I had an extra 20 years, I could learn web design, graphic design, writing, copywriting, accounting, and so on but as I said, I value simplicity so I hire the best and use my time to market my business more effectively.

In the past three years, I've sold The Coaching Academy and started another very successful company, SuccessTrack, which shows business owners how to create the business of their dreams – more profit, in less time with less effort. I bring together recognized experts on business growth, internet marketing, public relations and sales and present intensive bootcamps where delegates leave with a strategy for transforming their business into a sales and marketing machine.

And I've founded and launched a free nationwide business network group called The National Alliance of Business Owners (NABO).

I share with all those business owners the same simple but highly effective ingredients that I've revealed here that help create real success in life: get expert help; find a great coach or mentor; simplify your life; if you run a business, make sure you give people what they really want and follow in the footsteps of successful people.

In *Ultimate Life Lessons,* one of the UK's leading Success Coaches, Eve Grace-Kelly and her co-authors have skillfully produced an inspiring feast from experts in coaching and business that contains all of those ingredients and more and which will give you a highly-motivating, life-changing read. Dip into it today and discover how you can achieve all that you dream of.

Here's to your success!

Jonathan Jay,

Chairman NABO & SuccessTrack

www.NABO.biz

# Your Personal Mission Statement

Your Personal Mission Statement:

- Is your Personal Charter...
  - ▫ *Who you are*
  - ▫ *What you are*
  - ▫ *What you value*
- Forms the basis for making...
  - ▫ *Daily decisions*
  - ▫ *Major life-directing decisions*

Every one of the co-authors of this book has their own Personal Mission Statement. This has helped them get to where they are in life and their careers.

Consider the following when writing your own Personal Mission Statement:

1. Break your mission statement down into your roles in life (e.g. employee, colleague, parent, child, friend, manager, neighbor, etc., etc.) and the long-term goals you want to accomplish in each of those roles.

2. Now imagine that you are at your retirement party or your own funeral, and four people are going to speak about you. There will be one member of your family; one of your friends; one person from your work or profession; and one from a community organization that you are involved in.

- What would you like each of these speakers to say about you and your life?

- What character would you like them to have seen in you?

- What contributions and achievements would you want them to remember?

- What difference would you like to have made in their lives?

Visit www.QCCGroup.com/mission for your free workbook with further information on how to create your Personal Mission Statement.

# CONTENTS

# 12 ½ Principles Of Success
# - Common Traits Of
# Successful People

Have you ever had an area of your life you wanted to change (be it professional or personal), and even though you were committed to making that change, you still didn't do it? Why does this happen? What prevents you from making that change? Is it because you don't know how to?

We can all list a variety of reasons why we don't follow through on what we say we want to do, but the fundamental reason is down to our mindset. Research shows that 80% of success in anything is psychology, and only 20% is mechanics. The psychological part also needs to be aligned with our goals.

Success is not something that only a chosen few can achieve – it's available to all of us, in every area of our lives. You just need to know how to do things in such a way as to make sure you succeed every time. Many experts agree that success comes as a result of forming and repeating certain habits, with consistency being the key ingredient.

Dr Napoleon Hill, author of the bestseller Think and Grow Rich, pioneered the idea that successful individuals share certain qualities. He also asserts that examining and emulating these qualities can guide you to extraordinary achievements.

If you want to change an area of your life, follow the 12½* key Principles of Success in this book, learn from our co-authors' real-life lessons, and you will be able create sustainable and lasting change.

Remember, knowledge is only powerful if you act on what you know.

*"Nurture your mind with great thoughts,*
*for you will never go higher than you think."*
Benjamin Disraeli

* We say there are 12½ for those who are superstitious!

Eve Grace-Kelly, Success Coach, Author

# Open Your Mind – Get To Know Yourself

Every once in a while, we need to see ourselves from different perspectives and angles that we would not otherwise see. In Neuro Linguistic Programming (NLP) we call this 'Different Perceptual Positions.'

What you think and how you perceive a situation can be very, very different from someone else's perception of that same situation.

Explore a different view of yourself with the following exercise. You'll gain a deeper insight into you, which can lead you to take action or to accepting yourself just as you are.

To do this, you need to be open-minded and curious. It helps you to explore your memories and beliefs.

**Don't dwell long on each question. Read each one and quickly write down 5** answers to each question - whatever comes to mind.

1.  What five words describe you?

2.  What five objects have meaning for you?

3.  What feelings describe you?

4.  What five colors have meaning for you?

5.  What five places have meaning for you?

6.  What habits describe you?

7.  What words would you use to describe your mother?

8.  What words would you use to describe your father?

9.  What words would your mother use to describe you?

10. What words would your father use to describe you?

11. What words would you use to describe your spouse, partner, or best friend?

12. What words would you use to describe your enemies?

13. What words would your spouse, partner, or best friend use to describe you?

14. What words would your enemies use to describe you?

15. What beliefs describe you?

16. What else describes you?

So, what did you learn about yourself? Were there any surprises?

You can explore this exercise even further by asking your partner, parents, brothers, sisters, friends, colleagues, etc. to complete it for you. It can be quite an enlightening journey.

Eve Grace-Kelly, Success Coach, Author

# What Can We Learn From A Bear With A Small Brain?

Years ago, when I was teaching project management for a client, I used to include A A Milne's story about Edward Bear (aka Winnie the Pooh) to demonstrate a point.

It goes like this:

*"Here is Edward coming downstairs now, bump, bump, on the back of his head, behind Christopher Robin. It is, as far as he knows, the only way of coming downstairs, but sometimes he feels that there really is another way, if only he could stop bumping a moment and think of it."*

The story about him bumping down the stairs often strikes a chord with me, and I have also used the story in my coaching.

At first sight, it may not seem possible that we could share characteristics with a bear of little brain!

As Edward Bear bumps his head painfully down the stairs behind Christopher Robin, he gets a brief glimpse of a different reality. Between each bump on his head, he briefly sees a different way of doing things. But then the next bump comes along, and so Edward Bear doesn't get enough time to think about how he can better do things.

Many people can relate to the same experience – in both our personal lives and in our careers or businesses. We bump slowly down hill, bump, bump, bump. Once in a while, we may realize that there is another way of doing things. But then other things in life and work get in the way. The To-Do list is ever growing; the chores are mounting up.

Reading between the lines, we can see that Edward Bear really knows that there is a better way of getting downstairs – he just needed time to think about what that would be. So it is with us. Sometimes, we need to take time out and think.

So we invite you to take time out and read this book. Read about the experiences and life lessons of people who have stopped bumping down the stairs, and thought about what they were going to do to be a success in their lives.

**What can you do to stop the bumping in your life, your career, your business?**

The bumping will probably stop eventually anyway, but at what cost? When your business fails? When you lose your job? When your relationship fails?

So why wait? Take time out to think and get creative. Discover new ways to do what you do.

If you've read this particular story of Winnie the Pooh, you'll know that he does actually find himself a 'thinking spot'. In Piglet, he finds a coach, who asks him no end of questions.

---

*Exercise:*

*Do you feel there must be a better way of doing something that you're finding very challenging right now?*

*Do you have a coach or a support group who could help you make the changes you want in your life?*

*Make a difference... take action and find your Piglet!*

---

www.QCCGroup.com

*"The potential of the average person is like a huge ocean unsailed, a new continent unexplored, a world of possibilities waiting to be released and channelled towards some great good."*
Brian Tracy

Tracy Repchuk, #1 Woman Speaker in the
World for Internet Marketing

# Give Yourself A CHANGENDECTOMY

After spending 22 years as a successful entrepreneur, I realized one day that I didn't enjoy what I was doing. I was approaching my 40th birthday at the time, and I thought to myself if I don't start doing what my purpose or passion is in life now, when will I do it? From that day onwards - everything changed.

**Life lesson - change is for the better.**

It's funny how some people like things to stay the same - the status quo, so to speak. The laws of nature though say things must either go up or go down - they don't stay the same. It takes great effort to go up, most things go down by gravity alone, and all of it is considered a change. Time itself is a measure of change. Many think change will disrupt their lives, cause something bad to happen, require them to learn new skills or invest more time into something.

If you feel like this about anything - I say it's time for a *changendectomy* - removal of the fear of change.

I think what is perceived in life is that change *happens* to people; an illness strikes, a job is lost, a spouse leaves, kids move out, people die so we start thinking change is bad. And many of those things can be, and are - but... what if you had the ability to look at ALL change as for the better.

Guess what happens? You see far more good in change, and change becomes fun, exciting and a never-ending adventure of opportunities.

It is really a matter of perspective, and I don't say that to the point that when a person close to you dies, that's good - but what if you could find 'the silver lining' as they used to say - or simply say – *"well I don't know what is just around the corner but I know it's going to be for the better."* I could cite many examples of people's experiences I have watched - a spouse dies, and for the first time they are traveling - they get struck with an illness - and they are closer than ever to their family - a job is lost - and now they have the courage to start their own business. I myself have even experienced change that, at the time, sure didn't feel good - but when I look back now with 20/20 hindsight - it was often for the better.

By knowing change is for the better it makes it easy to accept, take advantage of, embrace, and best of all - not fear it.

So if you have ever heard the saying "Animals can smell fear", I think the same goes for change. If you fear something, you ultimately attract it, almost as a test until one day you say *"I'm not afraid of something"* and then you are no longer plagued by it.

Since I changed my attitude from change is a pain and always seems to happen when I least want or expect it - to I love change - my life has CHANGED.

And primarily because I create change - it no longer just happens to me. ♣am a cause of change.

- I said I'm going to CHANGE my job and career - and now I love what I do

- I said I'm going to CHANGE my attitude about the publishing industry - and I became a bestselling author

- I said I'm going to CHANGE my habits, and learn a whole new skill - and that resulted in me becoming the #1 woman in internet marketing in the world

- I said I'm going to CHANGE my lifestyle from being a homebody - and now I get paid to travel all around the world - and average 87 speaking invitations a year, in 22 countries

- I said I'm going to CHANGE my look - and I feel more alive and vibrant

- I said I'm going to CHANGE where I live - and I went from Toronto, Canada to Burbank, California - sun, sun, sun

Now, I seek out change like a missile, constantly in search of the opportunity that will bring about the biggest change, which results in the biggest rewards.

Some may call this risk-taking, and maybe causing change is a form of taking risks, but if that is the case - then all I can say is, by embracing both aspects, my life has made such big quantum leaps, that I'm now describing it with the word EPIC.

Change can be EPIC - so enjoy the journey and I'll see you on the other side.

www.MillionaireMarketingMiracles.com

Bev James, Managing Director of The
Coaching Academy, Co-Founder and CEO of
Entrepreneurs' Business Academy

# True Value Doesn't Always Come From Putting A Price Tag On Everything You Do

Sometimes in life and in work we should take up new opportunities
when they present themselves and take the chance to create our own
luck. I've felt the positive benefits of following this course of action
many times in my own life; but one experience literally changed the
course of my career.

In 2005, I was encouraged to attend a coaching weekend presented
by The Coaching Academy (TCA). I didn't particularly want to go
and went along only to support a friend who was keen to train with
them. However, the passion and commitment shown towards us by
TCA coaching trainers impressed me so much – that I signed up and
committed to training to become a certified coach. It isn't something
I had planned for myself, but this immensely positive experience
showed me something that I resonated with – and that I genuinely
wanted to do!

Over the next three months, I offered my time and my help for free
at TCA two-day introductory events and I gave up my weekends so
I could listen and learn from the speakers. In exchange for my time,
I was able to develop my coaching skills by listening to and working
with new coaches. In a very short period of time I became so well
known to the team that I was asked to present for TCA and I delivered
my first session for them soon after. It was called 'Turning Your Passion
into a Profession'.

Very soon afterwards, I achieved my dream of joining an elite team
of professional trainers. Their commitment had attracted me in

the first place, and my willingness to give my time allowed me the chance to demonstrate my passion for their business and to join their organization. (My business expertise was relevant too of course.) The first chapter of this story led, 1,000 days later, to November 2008, when I was appointed Managing Director of TCA.

Life lessons for not putting a price tag on everything we do:

- **Pay it forward:** My philosophy is always to give before you get when building a new business relationship. Giving makes you feel good and will make your associates feel valued and appreciated. It may be something simple like a business contact; it could be something greater like a discount or a complementary product or service. Giving before you get and putting aside the price tag, helps to create a climate of good will – in which loyalty develops and even better things will happen.

- **Show appreciation to others**: Whether to your clients, your staff, your boss or your family. Saying thank you, smiling, saying good morning, giving credit where it is due, and showing an interest in other people, will cost you nothing – and yet will pay you back many-fold. The majority of people come to work because they enjoy the company of their colleagues. It is more important than earning more money – although a pay rise is always welcome too! You can increase staff loyalty and reduce staff turnover simply by helping people to feel wanted and appreciated at work.

- **Encourage others to learn and grow**: Brief your people well – and then let them get on with the task. Review and appraise their work, so that they can learn more about what you want and expect from the feedback, but show them trust and respect – and encourage an ownership mentality. Once they know how much you care about the business and about their role in your business, your attitude towards the business and your customers will be reflected in theirs towards you.

- **Give away something for free**. When you set up a marketing campaign or rent a mailing list, don't begin by trying to sell something to make a profit. Focus instead on gaining contacts, names and addresses. Give away something for free and you often get much more back in the long run.

- **When we say 'yes' to life, we create our own luck**: My friend was a catalyst for getting me to the first training session at TCA. Had I said 'no thanks', I'd have missed the signpost and the opportunity.

- **When we have a passion for what we do, we become 'on purpose'**: Having a sense of purpose in our work keeps us connected to our core self. Doing what we love to do as much as possible isn't hard work, it's a pleasure.

- **Visualization is a key for success**: When you acknowledge to yourself what your real intention is, and what you want to achieve, you will move toward the goal, and the opportunity to achieve it will arrive.

---

*Exercise:*

*Where in your life have you missed an opportunity and regretted it?*

*What was the impact?*

*What are you going to do differently to embrace life and the opportunities that come your way?*

*When will you begin?*


*Where in your business life would 'giving before you get' make a difference?*

*What impact could it have?*

*What are you going to do differently in future?*

*When will you begin?*

---

www.BevJames.com


*"Think BIG! You are going to be thinking anyway, so think BIG!"*
Donald Trump

Penny Power, Founder of Ecademy.com, Social Networking Expert, Author

# Being You Is Enough

I have spent 46 years with the most extraordinary internal dialogue. I talk to myself endlessly and I am my biggest critic. I was told at the age of 19 by my first boss *"Penny, I don't need to manage you; you are the hardest boss anyone could have for herself"*.

My drive in life is one of constant improvement so that I can be a better person for others. I am a supporter and I love to empower others. I see these traits in one of my children and, through watching him grow up, I have seen myself - and I have wanted to learn to love myself more and be gentler with myself.

As a child I was told I was too sensitive; in business I was told I was too emotional; as a friend I am told I am too soppy; as an Aunty I was told I wanted too many hugs! I listened and I tried to adapt to all this 'constructive' feedback. And then, one day, a light went on in my head. It was as a result of helping someone else who was trying to adapt to everyone else at the expense of themselves.... I said to him *"Do you know, being you is enough"*.

I had no idea how empowering this statement was until that person wrote to me and told me I had changed their life as a result of these four simple words. Since then I have written about it, used it in training and speaking and have used this as an anchor for myself.

Say it to yourself *"Being me is enough"*. Watch how your shoulders slowly drop down from the tension of trying to be what everyone else wants you to be. When you do this, you will start to see how wonderfully unique and gorgeous you are and all that uniqueness will become your biggest asset in life. Stop pretending, and start being you. That is a liberating moment; feel it.

Why is this so important in today's world? Because the world is becoming transparent; people are becoming brilliant at reading other people's truths and intentions. In today's world, your personal brand is far more critical than your company brand. Building trust is about building trust in who you are. You are who you are.

---

*Exercise:*

This exercise comes from Dr Wayne W. Dyer's book – 10 Secrets for success and happiness.

*Point at yourself…. do it now.*

*What are you pointing at?*

*You will be pointing at your heart.*

*Your heart is who you are and is what people love about you, and that is the real you.*

*So what is on your heart?*

*Write down the words that you hear from your heart.*

*And now say to yourself, "Being me is enough".*

---

www.Ecademy.com

*"In April we cannot see sunflowers in France, so we say the sunflowers do not exist. But the local farmers have already planted thousands of seeds and when they look at the bare hills they may be able to see the sunflowers already.*
*The sunflowers are there. They lack only the conditions of sun, heat, rain, and July. Just because we cannot see them does not mean they do not exist."*
Thich Nhat Hanh

Emma Harrison, Owner and Founder of A4e

# Against All Odds…

I have made a TV show called *Who Knows Best?* in which I help an amazing young man called John find his first job.

My A4e staff knows that certain traits are often to be found in someone who has been unemployed for a long time: low confidence, low self-esteem, depression, anger, resignation and a feeling of not being wanted. When I met John, all these traits were there, plus many more.

What you don't see in 48 minutes of TV is the six weeks spent talking and listening, meeting his family, gaining his trust, venturing out into the world - work experience, volunteering, eating together, dealing with court papers, money, benefits, family issues, issues that pop up from the past, many job interviews, walking the high streets, introducing John and his résumé to employers, etc. etc.

John had been 'drifting' into a 'bad' way of life - he shyly told me he wanted to be 'booted and suited' and that now he had given up his bad way of life, he wanted to do the right thing - but he hated the thought of becoming a manual laborer - which is all 'people' expected him to be.

He had no qualifications whatsoever - but he knew he was bright. Very bright. I knew it too - his mathematical abilities blew me away and his ability to retain and adapt information was at a level I have rarely seen.

I had my work cut out. A young man - no work track-record - no qualifications - a 'bad boy' reputation - but hey - gorgeous, charming, humble and so, so keen to get on. Frankly - by the time John and I had worked together, everyone I introduced him to wanted him, including the staff at my own company A4e, who were all set to offer him a job!

If you've watched the program - you will know John got his first job and his dream. Booted and suited and on his way to becoming a forensic accountant on the 26th floor of a glass tower in the City of London. He is adored by his work colleagues - he says he has found his home.

When, on his first day at work, he was shown to his desk and his name appeared on the computer screen, he cried. I cried too.

The best tears of my year.

www.MyA4e.com

*"When the truly great people discover they have been deceived by the signposts along the road of life, they just shift gear and keep going."*
Nido Qubein

Gill Fielding, International Public Speaker,
Writer, Presenter, Mentor

# The Financial Recipe

I am often asked if there is one magic secret to creating wealth – and sadly there isn't. Creating wealth personally and in your business isn't easy. However, it can be simple – and the fundamental secret to wealth is to **spend less and invest more** – but most people find this incredibly hard to do and they hope that, rather than doing anything time consuming or difficult, that there may be an easy and immediate fix. There isn't – and if there were – everybody would be doing it!

However, I find that most people get put off too easily and imagine the pain of controlled wealth creation being far more than it actually is, and I have discovered that, if we turn some fundamentals of wealth creation into a formula or recipe that we follow all the time, then some of the wealth creating habits we need become habitual, easy and eventually enjoyable!

Almost every wealthy person that has ever lived follows these recipe steps:

- **Control the flow** of money through your life. Like any good recipe you need to rigidly measure what goes in and what goes out until you are experienced enough to 'judge' by eye and control the flow innately.

- **Layer it on** – and by that I mean keep adding to your inflow and keep re-investing any profit or surplus you make – until eventually the wealth is sufficient to sustain you forever.

- **Get control of debt** – understand it, use it and manage it.

- **Persist** – you have to keep going and keep tweaking your personal financial recipe until you can create wealth any time.

- **Grasp every opportunity you can** – and practice everything you do until it becomes a 'fine art'.

- *Balance* – make sure your money is split into different things and at different risk profiles – invest in a spread of things.

- *Make the money flow passively* into your life, with the least effort from yourself.

Like all great recipes, the more you practice this, the 'luckier' you will get and you will find that your wealth creation becomes easier and easier.

---

*Exercise:*

*Using the above points to guide you, review your financial profile and identify areas that could be improved. Are there any areas that you are having a problem with? If so, you might like to consider seeking out a financial coach to help you address what's holding you back.*

---

To read more about the financial recipe, have a look at: www.RichesTheMovie.com.

*"Money never starts an idea; it's the idea that starts the money".*
Mark Victor Hansen

# Success Principle #1:
# Adopt A Positive Mental Attitude

- This is the single most important success principle you could have. Without it, you won't achieve the maximum benefit from the other principles.

- As can be attested by the co-authors throughout this book, a positive mental attitude actually attracts opportunities for success. An upbeat attitude ensures your actions and thoughts steer you in the right direction to achieve your goals. It will also reduce your stress and have a helpful impact on your physical health.

- If you have a negative attitude, you are more likely to undermine your own efforts.

- A negative mental attitude repels opportunities and does not take advantage of them when they do come along, or even recognize an opportunity when it is presented.

- An optimistic person will find a way to get something done, whilst someone with a negative outlook will find reasons why something can't be done.

- The good thing is that your mental attitude is something over which you, and only you, have complete control!

- Five behavioral habits to practice and adapt to help the positive change you are looking for are:

  - **Create a positive environment**: The way in which you think forms the foundation of your attitude. Think in terms of positive thoughts, and your outward mood will reflect this. Do not wait for something good to happen to create this positive change for you; rather create the change by altering the way you think.

  - **Do not give up**: From time to time, life will present you with setbacks, but it is up to you as to how you choose to deal with them. If you view these setbacks as lessons to be learned, you are more likely to reach your goal as opposed to giving up.

- **Live in the moment**: Do not worry about what happened yesterday (it's gone) or what will happen tomorrow (there's still time to change things). Relish the good and the beauty of every moment as it occurs.

- **Expect good things**: Believe that you deserve good things and learn to expect the best out of every situation. This will lift your mood and you will become more attractive to others due to the feelings you radiate. A mutual positive outlook in any type of relationship will dramatically increase your well-being and also your chances of success.

- **Laugh**: Find humor in whatever you can. Laughter automatically puts a smile on your face and makes you feel good inside.

*Success attracts success - failure attracts more failure*

*"Minds are like parachutes –*
*they only function when open."*
Thomas Dewar

Debbie Allen, The Millionaire Entrepreneur
Business Builder

# Discovering And Developing Your Life's Purpose

*"Strive to be your best and then share your gifts*
*and talents in the service of others."*
*Debbie Allen*

How are you best utilizing your talents, knowledge and creative wisdom to inspire and help others? Why are you here? I discovered that I am a leader and an inspirational teacher. At first, I didn't really accept myself as a teacher. I knew I was a speaker and a writer, but I hadn't really realized that being a teacher was my purpose, and that's what I was put on this earth to do. Now I know that my passion has really been discovered, and that's what I will continue to do for the rest of my life.

*What series of events led to my discovery?*

I am passionate about speaking and teaching people how to have successful businesses. I've been doing this for twelve years, seven of them being full-time. Yet, it only became clear that this was my life's purpose in the last few years. I attended a breakthrough workshop with a mentor for two days, and it just hit me like a lightning bolt, *"This is what I was put on this earth for"*. The reason I had been doing all these other things in my life, such as building and selling businesses, was to get the expertise and the knowledge to do what I was really put on this earth to do - to teach others.

Now, my teachings are not just about business, they also include inspiration for personal growth and development. My presentations deal with mental belief systems and inner work. I discovered that teaching in this way is really my true gift. Others now receive my message from multiple angles, and it is such a blessing! I was innately transitioning into that type of work, but I didn't completely realize it until I refocused my life's intentions. Before my discovery, there was something missing for me, something I needed to be more passionate about.

**How to discover your life's purpose**

You cannot fully be of service to other people until you are of service to yourself. To do this, you need to be true to yourself and never settle for less than you deserve. Never stop learning and expanding personally. Be a life-long student, not just a student of what you think you have to learn in your industry. Become a life-long student learning more about YOU.

When you work on yourself inwardly, emotionally and psychologically, along with continually learning new business skills, that's when you really become a true master. That's when you become the best that you can be.

www.DebbieAllen.com

*"If there are a hundred steps in your path to success and you have not reached it in ninety-nine of them, do not conclude that the journey is a failure. Press on and up. The prizes are generally at the end of an effort, not at the beginning. And not to go on is to miss them. Be valiant... have faith in yourself. Success belongs to him who dares to win it."*
George S Forest

Eve Grace-Kelly, Success Coach, Author

# Move Away From The Conditioned Mind

*"To fear is one thing. To let fear grab you by the tail
and swing you around is another."*
Katherine Patterson

Why do we make the choices we do? Why is it that one person can persevere and do whatever it takes to achieve their goals while others remain seemingly trapped in a situation for years, unable to break the shackles that are holding them back?

Have you ever heard (or even said) something like "he's in his own little world!"? I heard this the other day while sitting on a train on a business trip to Paris….. not a bad place to do business! I've heard it often before (and even said it myself), but this time, it really got me thinking about how conditioned we can be in our own unique little world - the way we perceive and experience things are unique to us and no-one else. We are 'conditioned' by the way we grew up, by the values and beliefs we develop as part of our environment (people and things), by the limitations we were given or adopted, by the emotions we experience, by the attitudes, and opinions we experience.

As a child, I was very shy. This shyness affected me in all areas of my life to the extent that I didn't really have many expectation of myself in terms of what I could achieve. It wasn't really until I was in my twenties that I started to come out of my shell and become my own person. Maybe because, by then, I had a child to look after. I was someone he looked up to and expected comfort and reassurance from. I was someone he believed in, so not believing in myself was not an option!

Beliefs are one of the ways in which we organize our experience. They help us to make sense of the world we live in and to make predictions about what is going to happen. For example, I believe that the sun will rise tomorrow. However, until the sun actually comes up over the horizon, then this belief is really a prediction. Now, this belief is one that is universally shared and has a lot of evidence to back it up! Nonetheless, it is a belief.

I refer to beliefs as "childhood tapes" that play over and over again in our heads and often dictate our behavior. Do you recognize any of the following tapes?

- "It would be foolish and irresponsible to pursue my dreams"

- "It's no use applying for that promotion because I don't think I have what it takes to do the job"

- "I'm not smart enough to set up and run my own company"

- "I'm too old to go back to school and start a new career"

- "I'd better stay in this relationship – I'll never find anyone else who will love me"

- "I should never quit my job without having another one"

This conditioning affects everything we do and our every outlook on life.  It's a kind of distortion, similar to looking through a curved window.

With over 6 billion people in the world, that's a lot of individual worlds and a lot of curved windows!

This conditioning has an incredibly powerful influence on how we perceive ourselves and the choices we make. Ultimately, it has a huge impact on whether we are able to reach our maximum potential.  In effect, it is 'belief imprisonment'.

Clients often come to me saying they want to make a positive change in their lives or careers, but have struggled to take concrete actions to accomplish their goals. They are intelligent people and are motivated to make the change, but they are paralyzed by intangible inner obstacles.

Limiting beliefs almost always begin with the words "I can't because…" As soon as you say the word 'because' you invoke a part of your brain that believes, "I have a reason." (Example: "I won't get a promotion because I don't have the right qualifications.").  The effect is that you stop trying. If you continue to tell yourself you can't do something because…, you never will.

However, recognizing the effect our conditioning has is a huge first step to being able to make any changes necessary to break through any barriers (or distortions).  We can now start to see things in a different light.  We start to understand the impact these beliefs, values, emotion, attitudes and opinions have had on our own decisions and why they have often felt incongruent to us.  When this happens a phenomenal thing happens.  Things click into place.  Any anger that we experience starts to drift away because we now understand why we feel angry – we understand that the conditioning has distorted our views.  Our experience of life improves, and keeps on improving!

A story about limiting belief:

> The Pike is a large freshwater fish that preys on smaller fish such as minnows for its food. So, you would think that if a Pike is placed in a large tank of water with a lot of minnows he would be happy and well-fed Pike!
>
> However, in an experiment involving the study of animal behavior, a psychologist placed a Pike in a large tank that was divided into two by a glass barrier.  On one side of the glass was the Pike, and on the other side was a school of minnows. The Pike could see the minnows but every time that he tried to get them, he bumped into the glass barrier. As a result, he gave up trying as he was convinced that it was impossible for him to get at the minnows.
>
> Eventually, the glass barrier was removed.  However, the minnows were able to swim around with the Pike without being eaten by him. You see, the Pike did not believe that he could eat these minnows. His limiting belief was causing him to starve in the midst of plenty.

We are able to shake off the shackles of our conditioning and continue to grow and improve – to reach our maximum potential.  It might seem a bit frightening at first because it's sometimes easier to stay as we are, to continue to accept our conditioning and all of the limitations that it holds for us.  There's an element of security in that conditioning.

But if you want to make changes in your life, take advantage of this learning.  Recognize that you have the power within you to **BE More – DO More – ACHIEVE More™.**

We all have within us the potential to be our very, very best. We just need to take a little bit of a risk now and then to step outside of our comfort zone and to experience the freedom it can give us.

So how do you take break through these limiting beliefs?

---

*Exercise:*

*Below are some common limiting belief types. Which ones could be holding you back from achieving your goals? Do you think…..?*

- *I'm worthless – If you feel worthless or undeserving, you may fail to notice what you're good at.*

- *It's useless – If you don't see something as desirable, you may view it as useless. However, most events have both a short-term and long-term result. If you only focus on short-term results, you could miss an opportunity.*

- *It's hopeless – When you think something isn't possible, you won't even try to do it.*

- *I'm helpless – When you don't know how to do something or, you start to feel helpless and unable to resolve your situation. The goal or the steps involved seem too difficult, and this results in you giving up.*

- *I'm blameless – If you find yourself blaming external events or situations, you are taking the easy and, perhaps, lazy way out. Once the current external event is over, you'll quickly find something else to blame for your situation!*

*Now, question your belief/s: For example:*

- *If you believe "I'm worthless," ask "How do I deserve it?"*

- *If you believe "It's useless," ask "How is it desirable?"*

- *If you believe "It's hopeless," ask "How is it possible?"*

- *If you believe "I'm helpless," ask "What do I already know about it?"*

- *If you believe "I'm blameless," ask "How am I responsible?"*

*Finally, test your new thinking.  Take a limiting belief you have and
turn it around and test it. For example, suppose your limiting belief
is "I can't get the promotion I want because I don't have the right
qualifications." You would test that by asking yourself, "How would
not having the qualifications make it easier to get the promotion?"
or "How would obtaining the qualifications make it difficult to get
the promotion?" You may realize that many people work their
way up quickly through a company but started out with little or no
qualifications.   If they didn't have the qualifications, how is it possible
for them to get promoted time and time again? Sometimes it's not the
qualification that count, it's the way in which you are motivated or
how you apply yourself.*

*The key is to change your thought process and thereby your belief
about a particular situation. Open your mind to new possibilities for
your situation.  You'll find that what seemed like a dismal circumstance
can instantly transform into endless opportunity.*

---

www.QCCGroup.com

*"When you change the way you look at things,
the things you look at change."*
Dr. Wayne Dyer

Stephanie Hale, Publishing Expert and
Writing Coach

# What If You Had Just Two Months?

Imagine this... You're sitting on a wooden bench in heavy rain. You have no umbrella. Your jacket is so wet, it's changed color. The rain thrums so hard against the pavement, it bounces.

You really should stand up and walk home – put on some dry clothes. But you're numb. You're mother of three beautiful kids. And you've just been told you might have a brain tumor. There's so much water dripping in your eyes, you can hardly see. You're thinking: "Is this it? Is this really it? Is this really, really it?"

This was me back in 2008. I was filled with regret at all the dreams that I'd put off for 'tomorrow'. I'd been so busy being busy that I'd neglected my 'todays'.

I had a two-month wait for my MRI scan. So I made a conscious decision to make the most of every precious second. During that time, I had fun days out with my kids; I spent special time with my parents; I reconnected with old friends. It was also the powerful motivating force to start writing my book *Millionaire Women, Millionaire You* and to launch The Millionaire Bootcamp for Women, in Earl's Court, London.

As it turned out, the MRI eventually revealed a rare brain condition that I'd had since birth. Nothing life-threatening. However, the experience was a blessing in disguise as it taught me the importance of living in my today!

Now imagine... if you had bad news and a two-month wait, what would you do? How would you spend your time? Is there anything you have put off doing till tomorrow? Are you truly living your dreams today?

---

*Exercise:*

*Write a list of all the goals and dreams you have for yourself.*

*Put them in priority order based on the ones that are most important to you.*

*Now, what are you going to do about those goals and dreams? How are you going to make them happen…..?*

---

www.MillionaireWomenMillionaireYou.com/free

www.MillionaireWomenResources.com

*"The people who get on in this world are the people who get up and look for the circumstances they want and, if they can't find them, make them."*
George Bernard Shaw

Kevin Green, Property Development Trainer

# You, Your Confidence And Your Gut!

During a scholarship, where I interviewed top entrepreneurs from Bill Gates to Richard Branson, one of the themes that stood out was that some of the most successful people in the world will often make decisions more from the heart than from the head.

After this research, I received a flyer inviting me to a seminar on property investment. Always the cynic, I went along ready to be dismissive. However, what I realized was that property was my future and I signed up for a long-term educational and mentorship package. This package gave me the confidence, knowledge and tools to go out and apply what I had learnt.

People underestimate the power of confidence. With confidence, you can do almost anything. And confidence, coupled with hard graft, a good team around you and a social conscience, are a winning mix.

For some reading my story, they may think I am just lucky. But, no-one achieves anything in life without hard work, commitment and making some mistakes along the way. But we all have choices in life, and that is what ultimately defines us.

As any entrepreneur will concur, passion drives a business, particularly in the first few years, and the use of phraseology like 'I love this logo' or 'I hate that website' might be regularly used in a business context, sometimes without us even realizing we are putting our hearts into the words. Yes, businesspeople need to focus on the bottom line, but most of us are guided by instinct and what makes our heart flutter – particularly at the moment, when the economic crisis has made us sit up and re-evaluate what is important to us.

**Life Lesson 1**: I am now an advocate of 'the gut reaction' in business and life, which may surprise some, given I am such a number cruncher.

**Life Lesson 2**: Gain the knowledge you need to take confident decisions in any area of life. This will give your head the support it needs in decision-making. Your heart / gut will do the rest!

*Exercise:*

*Next time you're faced with a business decision or a property purchase, consider this: you may have calculated the numbers for a particular business venture or buying a house, but listen to what your heart (your gut instinct) is also telling you. If the two chime, you could be on to a winner!*

www.KevinGreen.co.uk

www.PropertyTrain.biz

*"Don't let what you can't do stop you
from doing what you can do."*
John Wooden

Eve Grace-Kelly, Success Coach, Author

# Miscellaneous Life Lessons – Part I

Here are a few life lessons sent to us by a selection of our clients. Some of them come from deep within their hearts and have had a profound impact on their personal development, self-awareness, relationships and careers.

Which ones can you relate to? Which ones can you learn from? Tick those that apply and work on integrating the lessons into your own life.

| I've learned that................. | ✓ |
|---|---|
| .... you can keep going long after you can't. | |
| .... my best friend and I can do anything or nothing and have the best time. | |
| .... just because someone doesn't love you the way you want them to doesn't mean they don't love you with all they have. | |
| .... you shouldn't be so eager to find out a secret. It could change your life forever. | |
| .... even when you think you have no more to give, when a friend cries out to you, you will find the strength to help. | |
| .... you cannot make someone love you. All you can do is be someone who can be loved. The rest is up to them. | |
| .... it's not what you have in your life but who you have in your life that counts. | |
| .... you should always leave loved ones with loving words. It may be the last time you see them. | |
| .... it isn't always enough to be forgiven by others. Sometimes you have to learn to forgive yourself. | |
| .... we don't have to change friends if we understand that friends change. | |
| .... regardless of how hot and steamy a relationship is at first, the passion fades and there had better be something else to take its place. | |
| .... it takes years to build up trust, and only seconds to destroy it. | |

Susanne Jorgensen, Psychologist, Coach, Author

# Relationship Success... From The *Inside* Out

*"All change in your outer world begins with a change in your inner world"*
Brian Tracy

People spend a huge amount of their lives tantalized by love - either by looking for it, trying to keep it, or trying to get over it. We have more opportunities to meet people; we have more disposable income; more leisure time; more dating; and relationship advice, than any generation before, yet finding love still seems so elusive to so many.

The stereotypical dating behaviors that are encouraged for women include scheming, flattering, seducing and/or playing hard to get. The stereotypical behaviors encouraged for men are based on a model of love-seeking where the idea of romantic pursuit is a type of predation, a hunting experience – the goal of which is to capture. There are a myriad of books, websites, coaching courses, online forums and workshops that will teach you how to successfully 'hunt', 'lure', 'seduce', 'dominate or 'close the game.' The common thread is how to 'make' someone desire you, want you or love you.

The one thing these techniques have in common is that they are based on manipulation, ego stroking and game playing. Likewise they are built on a false premise – that we actually can 'make' someone fall for us. Are we really all that surprised then that we can't find meaningful and fulfilling relationships that last?

We want honesty; we want to trust; we want to be loved for who we are; yet we are engaging in a 'game' and treating each other with deceit, manipulation and in doing so, we are also wearing masks - pretending to be someone we aren't.

*"You must be the change you want to see in the world"*
Mahatma Gandhi, Indian political and spiritual leader (1869 - 1948)

The modern dating advice reminds me of the zillions of popular diet books that claim to be the solution to losing weight, while at the same time, obesity is on the rise!

I don't think it is difficult to see how the popular dating industry, like the dieting industry, isn't working. One only needs to look at the divorce statistics, look at the relationships of people you know, look at your own relationship history or look at the number of people who are on dating websites. Just listen to how many conversations take place every day about how people are fed up, frustrated with 'the dating game' and not being able to find happy and fulfilling relationships.

Einstein is credited for defining 'insanity' as *"doing more of the same and expecting a different outcome"*.

Don't you think it's about time we see all the modern hype about how to date, how to find the love of your life and 'live happily ever after' for what it really is? It's about fuelling a lucrative industry – it's not about what works in the real world for real people!!

Following Einstein's theory then, isn't it about time we rethink the dating 'game'?

- *Isn't about time we realize that the current model isn't working and that we start doing something different?*
- *Isn't it time to stop focusing on 'doing' and start focusing on 'being'?*
- *Isn't it time to stop focusing on the 'outside' job and start focusing on the 'inside' job?*

The way of thinking that leads to successful relationships has got to be altogether different than what is currently on offer.

In my own personal experience and in my experience as a psychologist and coach, I have found that the formula for happy, successful relationships happens from the 'inside-out' by:

Creating a successful
relationship with yourself

Creating a successful,
purposeful and fulfilling life

Attracting success, fulfilling
and happy relationships

The way to find love is to become so much yourself that you attract others of your own kind, with whom you can share this freedom.

The good news is that, no matter what your past has been, you can create a new ending to your relationship story – from the inside out. It all begins with YOU!

*Exercise:*

*Think about, and write down, your answers to the following two questions:*

- *Think of the kind of person you would like to be with - or*

- *Think of the kind of relationship you would like to experience*

*Try to be as specific as you can. What would you see, hear and experience? How would you know you were with that kind of person? How would you know you were having that kind of relationship?*

*Now take a few moments to think about and write your answers to the following questions:*

- *Who would you have to be, to attract that kind of person?*

- *What would be your part to have that kind of relationship?*

- *What is your next step towards achieving this?*

www.TheSinglesGym.com

www.SelectDatingServices.com

# Success Principle #2: Develop A Clear Vision

- As Debbie Allen found, in her Life Lesson: **Discovering And Developing Your Life's Purpose**: once she discovered her life purpose to be an inspirational teacher, she was able to define her vision – what she was *"....put on this earth for"*.

- Have a crystal clear vision of what exactly it is you want to achieve or become. It is a picture or idea you have in your mind of yourself, your business, or anything else you would like to happen. A clear vision will open your mind to the endless possibilities of the future.

- A vision is a strong force in anyone's life, but is essential in business. The continual presence of a vision helps to motivate against forces of resistance.

- Visions will help you to overcome obstacles in your way and help you persevere when times are tough.

- A well-defined vision helps you to focus and create a purpose that becomes a measurement for your success.

- Without a vision of who you want to be, how you want to succeed or what you want out of life, you lack drive and your life becomes just an order of events.

- Regularly review your vision statement to ensure you are still on track. Be open to change, but be clear as to why the change is needed.

- *Important things to remember when creating a vision:*

  1. Know exactly who you are

  2. Brainstorm, dream, and let your imagination be as creative as it can be

  3. Focus on things that give your life purpose and meaning

  4. Do not put limits on your dreams.

**Start with the end in mind**

Katie Moore, Entrepreneur, Investor

# "When Things Go Wrong, Don't Go With Them……."

Renée Locks

Seven years ago, I came across a greetings card with a big red ink splat on the front and the quote, *"When things go wrong, don't go with them……."* and since then, I have this card [still in its plastic wrapper] on display in a prominent part of my daily life - fridge door, dressing room mirror or by the front door. These wise words have prompted me into action on many occasions, for which I am eternally grateful!

Having an entrepreneurial spirit means that I am a bit of a risk-taker in every walk of life: I try to defy those risks by making calculated decisions; however, sometimes, things happen – and everything goes wrong. What should you do? How much effort should you put into something that is becoming increasingly obviously 'not working'?

There is no easy way to decide to call it a day. I know – I've been there! But learning from experiences and not making the same mistake twice, really helps! I try not to be so gullible but still to keep an open mind and heart; I plan for contingencies – what if this happens, or that happens? I try to understand more, plan more. All this helps.

Of course, you can't see into the future, but you can do as much as possible to make sure that things don't go wrong. So, regularly reading the quote, **"When things go wrong, don't go with them…….."** makes me grateful for the good things in life that are going well; reminds me to sharpen-up on current relationships; and makes me grateful that I chose to leave certain relationships behind!

Many relationships and businesses fail because of a lack of understanding. If this is the case, find out why and put things right. If you haven't set any controls or goals, then how do you know that things are going wrong? They do go wrong and it's a bit of a shock when it happens! You want to do all you can to make them better, but often it's too late. So in this instance......... *"When things go wrong, don't go with them........"*

Best to call it a day and let go.

---

*Exercise:*

*What are you holding on to that you know you should really let go of? Be honest with yourself!*

*By letting go of the things you can't control or change in your life, you allow people to be responsible for themselves, and this removes a tremendous burden off you.*

*You will then appreciate life more for what it is. Not only that, but you will have the strength and energy to pursue your own interests, relax and have fun.*

---

www.KatieMoore.co.uk

www.BusinessEssentialsAcademy.com

*"It's not so much what happens to us,
as what happens in us that counts."*
Tim Hansel

Janet Beckers, Internet Marketing Expert,
Speaker, Author, Mentor

# Often The Simplest Solution Is The Best

One of the things I love about entrepreneurs, is the excitement we bring to planning solutions to problems. We can see so many possibilities and exciting and challenging ways to tackle a project that it is very tempting to combine them all. When we do this, we tell ourselves we are: "over-delivering", "being creative", "being thorough" or even just plain old "being very clever".

This can be like combining too many different flavors in a recipe. The result is, instead of impressing our customers by over-delivering, we actually end up overwhelming them. Instead of giving them clarity on how we can help them, we instead leave them confused and not sure what to do first.

One of my biggest lessons in business has been to keep things simple. It takes a real maturity to resist the temptation to make things more complicated than they should be and instead opt for simple and elegant.

---

*Exercise:*

*Take an honest look at the way you are approaching your business and other areas in your life.*

*Are you complicating things?*

*Is there an alternative that is much simpler?*

*Be gentle with yourself and forgive yourself for your enthusiasm to over-deliver...then ruthlessly simplify!*

---

www.WonderfulWebWomen.com

Vinden Grace, Internet Business Specialist/
Digital Coach

# What's Left After The Honeymoon?

When you go through a divorce with (or rather against!) someone, you really learn about their character, their values, etc. In the heady bloom of a relationship's initial stages, we are sometimes blind to the fact that two or three years down the road, once the honeymoon period of a marriage is over, the number of similar values between couples can be very small.

Research studies show that approximately one in three marriages sadly end in divorce. From our own observations, we find that couples with similar core values are more likely to care about, rather than just be attracted to, each other and get along well once that honeymoon phase passes. In relationships where couples argue about the same things over and over again, and don't seem to get anywhere with solving the problems, you will see different core values, and it's the conflict between these core values that is causing the argument. There have also been numerous scientific studies with regard to the theory of our psychological needs, our values and personality traits. Some research shows how the motivational spectrum produces different personality traits and values, and how that correlates to the way we handle/deal with our personal relationships.

We all have a number of core values by which we live. They make us who we are. They define us. Over time, the importance of these values can change, but rarely do the actual values change. What generally happens is that we start to notice that our values are different to those of our partner, or that our values are not being honored. We then either expect the other person to change their values or we consider changing our own, which is difficult in many ways, as we each believe that living a life that honors our values leads to our greatest happiness.

We can change our behavior. We can be tolerant. But this doesn't change our underlying values. All that happens is that our tolerance creates distance from the other person. Of course, we can agree to disagree! This demonstrates respect for the other person's set of values. But it can also mean that we are going in different directions if the values are not compatible.

Understanding each other's values, and how they are shared, creates a bond between us and creates a deep sense of understanding each other.

It's important to take on board the lesson that, just because a relationship didn't work, it didn't mean that, personally, we are failures: simply that the relationship was the thing that didn't work in the long-term. People change and sometimes do so in opposite, or at least different, directions and they can therefore drift apart, realizing that they hold different values and wanting different things from life. It's sad, but it happens. A new life awaits….with someone whose values are more closely aligned to yours.

---

*Exercise:*

*Do you know what your values are?*

*If you are experiencing problems in a relationship, whether it's with your partner, friend, colleague, etc., carry out a values elicitation exercise to see where the differences lie.*

*Before entering into a relationship with someone, especially a long-term one as serious as marriage, check to see whether both parties' values are similar. This is well worth doing at any stage of a relationship to ensure that you have common ground for the future.*

*Visit www.QCCGroup.com/personalcoaching for a **free** workbook on how to find out what your core values are.*

---

www.ANewYouAfterDivorce.com

*"When one door of happiness closes, another opens. But often we look so long at the closed door that we don't see the one which has opened."*
Helen Keller

Peter Thomson, Business and Personal Growth Strategist

# Where Success Lives

It's strange how some people grasp it and some still don't. Perhaps, even more peculiar, is that some never understand and yet others grasp it without even trying.

More perplexing still – once they're older, then almost, yes, I must qualify this, <u>almost</u> everyone finally understands.

You know, it's one of the true secrets of success. I wonder why it takes so long for so many to finally 'get it'. Do you think it's because they think success is NOT for them? Have they been conditioned by that societal mindset that indicates such a life is only for the privileged few? The lucky ones born into success, the 'fortunates' who stumbled across the secret never really deserving it? (According to many who don't stumble.)

Maybe, just maybe – the newspapers, the TV stations, the blaring radios of mind-numbing garbage are in cahoots to keep the vast majority of the population in the dark, in the sheep field of blandness, in the win-the-lottery-is-the-way-to-success mindset – just so they won't find out.

I found out one fortunate day when I said 'No' to a client and really meant it – and never looked back. I'm so pleased I did.

So, how will you discover the secret? Is it hidden in some dark dungeon that seldom sees the light of day? No! Is it disclosed in a best-selling video and book expounding 'mindset actually works'? Partly! Is it there on view for anyone with half a mind, or even perhaps a whole one, to see and understand it for themselves? YES! It certainly is.

Here it is for you... right here, right now, right this very second – are you ready to know? Read on....

To be successful in life, in business, in anything and everything – you have to live in a little village... just south of... arrogant! Oh so simple, oh so misunderstood!

Now be careful, this is NOT that town of COCKY. Oh no! It's certainly not the urbanization of ARROGANT. It's just 'south of arrogant', and 'north of confident' – in that place of sure-of-mind; sure-of-purpose; sure-of-self.

Would you like to live there too? Great! That's where you'll meet all the other successful people too – enjoy!

www.PeterThomson.com

*"Some people have thousands of reasons why they cannot do what they want to, when all they need is one reason why they can."*
Willis Whitney

Curly Martin, Founder of Achievement
Specialists, Author, Speaker

# Coach Yourself
# To Health

*"The first wealth is health"*
*Ralph Waldo Emerson*

For 38 years, I was convinced that I was infallible as far as my health
was concerned. I swam regularly, danced the weekends away, started
slimming diets regularly, ate out often, looked fit, and generally never
gave my health a second thought except when overcoming a winter
cold bout. This therefore translated to good health to me. My health
was so robust I worked 12-14 hour days filled with stressful peaks and
dull troughs whilst always feeling I had not done enough and often
feeling unsatisfactory.

Until, that is, I was diagnosed with an aggressive form of breast and
lymphatic cancer and given 9 months to live! Although this seemed to
be out of the blue, I realize now that I had been creating the perfect
environment for cancer.

Chasing wealth instead of health, simply because my health had
always been good; had always been there for me.

Let's cut right to the chase. How do you define your 'health?' Forget
the clichés that you may have heard in seminars or read in books.
A surprising number of people never actually think about and
plan their health. They drift along being buffeted by the marketing
advertisements, time of year, climate, what others are doing, and
finding themselves fat or thin, healthy or sick, without planning and
deciding what they want from health. Many people go from one meal
to the next and consider that walking to the shop for the lunchtime
sandwich is exercise. Is this you?

A fortunate few have found that if they planned their health early
in life and pointed their education towards a particular calling
or vocation, they could maintain a healthy life style because it is

important for them. Some people, at quite a late stage in their lives, made a major mid-life health switch and began looking at and thinking about health in very different ways. Others, like myself, wait until a significant physiological event before taking stock.

Several people simply picked up their attitudes to health from their family examples or from that of their friends, following what everyone around them does as far as health is concerned. Did YOU make the decisions about your health or were they made for you? Did you drift into your health routines? How do you feel right now about stopping the drift and taking some positive action to take control of your health, your life and your destiny? So the question to ask, and more importantly answer yourself, is how did you end up where you are now, health wise?

On a scale of 1 to 10 (where 10 means being fully committed to changing your situation and beliefs about health and taking action, and 1 means being not bothered), how committed are you to sorting out your health?

Already by now, you have discovered that coaching is about asking questions that you may not have considered before and finding answers that may surprise or delight you and that might even, in some cases, frighten you. This may be the first time in your life that you have given yourself permission to appear this selfish, introspective or self-interested.

If you could do absolutely anything as far as your health is concerned, without any limitations, with no possibility of failure and without having to answer to anyone else, what would you do about your health? Be as specific as you can as you consider all possible health areas you could be involved in. Some of my coaching clients cannot think about what they want health wise, they can only think about what they don't want to do. It is okay if you begin by thinking about what you do not want to do and then turn it around. So: 'I do not want to only eat salads all day' could turn to: 'I want to put healthy food regularly into my diet.'

What I want

What I don't want

It will help you to come up with possibilities if you also consider the most important benefits that you want your health to provide.

For example, which of these are most important to you - slim body, good skin texture, ability to run up stairs with breath to spare, relaxing time, fun filled exercising... and so on.

My benefits of good health are:

Once you understand what it means to you to be healthy, you can now decide what changes you may need to organize to ensure your continuing health. Write down 3 simple things you will do to improve your health. The sort of things my clients write are, replace biscuits with fruit, drink two pints of water a day, use the stairs at work rather than take the lift. I'm sure you get the picture. Simple, small and effective steps that are easy to start, easy to maintain. Over to you.

3 simple things I will do this week to improve my health:

1.

2.

3.

The life lesson for me?: Without my health, I have no wealth of life!

www.AchievementSpecialists.co.uk

Seema Sharma, Dentist, Entrepreneur, Philanthropist

# Get On The Bus Of Opportunity!

I'm a great believer in taking opportunities when they present themselves... they always lead to more opportunities, and I don't always start with the end in mind. How many times have you heard that you should do the opposite?

'Destination: a land of more opportunity' my grandparents must have typed into their satellite navigation system back in the 1920s, when they set sail for the unknown on a Dhow boat, leaving behind family, their village, India - and not knowing if they would ever return, or ever make it. I am delighted I inherited some of their entrepreneurial spirit and sense of adventure.

Every time I start cooking, I hope for the end product that the recipe promises, but many of my dishes don't end up quite like they looked in the picture in the recipe book – perhaps because of my low threshold for substituting the ingredients I do not have! I apply the same logic that I apply to my businesses - improvise as you learn!

My favorite dinner parties were ones that my parents used to have when they organized Rotary events in Zambia – they were called progressive dinners, with each course being a well kept surprise at a different Rotarian's house. I learnt at a young age that 'progressive' meant 'keep moving '!

I don't think I've ever really known what is in store for the next year or two, let alone what my final destination will be, but along the way I've set up several successful dental practices, masterminded several property renovation projects, built a medical training consultancy, Medibyte Ltd, and founded a dental training consultancy, Dentabyte Ltd.

And those were the side dishes...my husband and children remain central to everything I do.   I have certainly had a varied and fulfilling career, and made some varied and interesting meals for my husband and daughters at the same time!

Admittedly, my recipe for success has been to create a series of fortunate coincidences by being in the right place at the right time, and doing my homework, even if I don't always hand it in on time!

www.TheSharmaFoundation.org

www.medibyte.com

www.dentabyte.co.uk

www.SmileImpressions.com

*"By believing in yourself,*
*you open the door to the art of possibility.*
*By not believing in yourself,*
*you close the door to your own potential."*
Eve Grace-Kelly

# Success Principle #3:
## Believe In Yourself

- Believe that you will succeed.

- Professional athletes and their coaches know this, as Tony Garbett (see his Life Lesson: *Self-Belief*) attests to. Sports coaches know that, while the game's fundamentals and physical conditioning are essential to success, so is the correct mental state.

- Stay away from negative influences that make you doubt your ability to succeed.

- Surround yourself with things that remind you that you can, and will, succeed.

- You are a unique being. You have your own talents, abilities and amazing potential. Any limits on what you can achieve are largely self-imposed. As Stephanie Hale highlights in her Life Lesson: *Making A Breakthrough*, Roger Bannister clearly proved that by establishing *"a strong belief that it could be done, the 'impossible' became 'possible'."*

- Susanne Jorgensen says in her Life Lesson: *If You Believe...*, *"Your world is a hologram that is reflecting back to you whatever you believe."*

- Remember what Venus Williams, Olympic gold medalist and professional tennis champion said: *"You have to believe in yourself when no-one else does, that is what makes you a winner."*

- Make a habit of saying aloud what you want to achieve. It is important to say it in the present tense, e.g., "I am confident", as opposed to, "I will be confident". If, at first, you feel awkward about saying it aloud to yourself, write down the affirmation. Carry it around with you and look at it several times each day. Better still, find a quiet time and rewrite it, until you fill up a page. This helps your mind stay focused on the goal (see Success Principle #9: Stay Focused).

- Self-belief also builds your confidence. As Kevin Green found (see his Life Lesson: *You, Your Confidence And Your Gut!*), *"..confidence, coupled with hard graft, a good team around you and a social conscience are a winning mix".*

Eve Grace-Kelly, Success Coach, Author

# Adopt A Winning Mindset

*"Whatever the mind dwells on, the body reveals."*
*Stephen P King*

Even before I became a Neuro Linguistic Programming (NLP) Practitioner, I was interested in people's body language and the way that someone's physiology changed depending on how they felt.

During my time as a Human Resources professional, working at Fidelity Investments, I had a recruitment plan for 45 graduate investment trainees. With that many to recruit at a time when the company was growing so quickly, I had to be particularly mindful of taking an holistic view during the interview sessions. I had so many people to recruit that I would take home the résumés the night before the long days of interviews.

Not surprisingly, I wasn't always on top form when conducting the interviews and I noticed this in my questioning techniques and also in my body language. People are exceptionally intuitive (without knowing it most of the time) at reading the signals that we give out, and on one occasion during an interview, an interviewee asked me whether I was interested in hiring him or not. After I picked my jaw up from the floor, I realized that I wasn't giving him my full attention as much as I should have been. He was a fantastic candidate after all, but following a long night of résumé reading, I was tired, and it showed. And although I already knew that I wanted to hire him, my thought processes had already jumped to the next interview that I would have to conduct – one that I already had a gut feel that the person wouldn't fit. (Sometimes, it's not what people say in their résumé, it's what they don't say!)

Obviously, this showed in my body language and my current interviewee picked it up. That really started me on my journey of understanding the connection between someone's feelings and physiology.

After that day, I paid particular attention, not only to the body language of anyone I was dealing with (not just interviewees), but also other colleagues, managers, friends, family, etc. Even on TV. Now, I'm not much of a sports fan, apart from watching the occasional game of soccer or tennis, but have you ever noticed that when a player starts to lose, they adopt defeatist body language and a negative mindset? Their shoulders droop, they frown deeply, their head hangs low and they drag their feet between shots. Those who are winning have much more upbeat body language and a positive mindset. They are dancing from one foot to another, they punch the air with excitement, and they engage with the crowd a lot more.

Five frogs are sitting on a log. Four decide to jump off. How many are left?

See following page for the answer.

The right mindset of an athlete is critical to the outcome of their game. That's why they have coaches. To give them a winning mindset.

One of the exercises I use with coaching clients is what's called the 'Resistance Test'. Try this with a colleague, friend or family member, as it needs two people.

*Exercise:*

*Stretch out your less dominant arm in front of you. The other person should then place their hand on your extended forearm, and place their other hand on your shoulder/collarbone for stabilization. They should then ask you to resist as they apply gradually increased pressure.*

*Next, repeat the exercise, but this time, you should think of negative thoughts whilst holding out your arm. With these negative thoughts, say to yourself 'feeble and weak'. While continuing to think of these negative thoughts, your partner should press down on your forearm, and you should continue to resist the pressure.*

*Repeat the exercise for a third time, but this time think of positive thoughts whilst holding out your less dominant arm. This time, say to yourself 'powerful and strong'. Again, your partner should press down on your forearm, and you should resist the pressure.*

*What happened while you were resisting the pressure? What was the difference between the time you were thinking negative thoughts and the time you were thinking positive thoughts?*

*More often than not, what happens is that your resistance will be stronger when you have positive thoughts. You have a much stronger mindset and the inner strength that comes from this has a direct impact on your success.*

*Atheletes with a winning mindset train harder. They constantly develop their skills, but in both attitude and physical skills. So it is with all of us. having a winning mindset builds our confidence, our belief in ourselves, and our abilities. This also has a powerful impact on how we set our goals. They tend to be much more positively stated and ambitious.*

---

So the lesson here is, be aware of what you say and how you say it, both in the actual spoken word and the body language you exhibit while speaking or, indeed, listening. This will help you get more of what you want.

What was your answer to the five frogs riddle?

Well, the answer is five....... because there's a difference between deciding and doing. It's all down to your mindset.

www.QCCGroup.com

*"One machine can do the work of fifty ordinary men.
No machine can do the work of one extraordinary man."*
Elbert Hubbard

Toby Garbett, Olympian

# When Opportunity Knocks....

I believe life lessons aren't always set in stone, and depending upon what happens in your life, they may evolve as you get older. For me, at this point in time, one of my top four has to be –

## Opportunity

As you go through life, opportunities come in different forms and will sometimes pass you by very quickly. What you don't want is to be in a position to say, "I wish I had done that". Be proactive and when an opportunity arises, take it!

---

*Exercise:*

*Imagine yourself sitting in your rocking chair in your twilight years, looking back on your life. Are there any opportunities that came your way and then passed you by because you didn't seize them?*

*If so, why is this? Most people would say, "It wasn't the right time." Is this you? Could it be a touch of procrastination creeping in? One of the biggest mistakes people make is spending too much time looking for the big opportunity, or the perfect timing to do something.*

*Well, there's a thin line between patience and procrastination. Patience is taking a well-calculated risk, and taking the time to learn what to do. It's saying: " I'll finish this by ____".*

*Procrastination is about avoiding risk. It's knowing what to do, but not doing it! People who procrastinate say, "I'll get to it sooner or later – when I have time."*

*As my grandma always said: "Start cooking while the pot is hot!"*

*The best time to build momentum is when you first think of an idea or start on a task. This is when you should take some small steps and use these to measure your progress.*

*Opportunities don't disappear, they simply move on to the next recipient. An opportunity that comes your way could be one that someone else procrastinated about or passed on. If you pass up on a good opportunity, then someone else will capitalize on it.*

---

www.TobyGarbett.com

*"Life's ups and downs provide windows of opportunity to determine your values and goals - Think of using all obstacles as stepping stones to build the life you want."*
Marsha Sinetar

*"Opportunity dances with those who are already on the dance floor."*
Jackson Brown

Marie O'Riordan, Communications Excellence
Specialist

# Health Is Wealth

Please ask yourself right now and read aloud with me the next sentence...

*"What can I do right now, in this moment, to prove to myself that my Health is my Wealth?"*

I've lived with chronic to acute migraine since birth and I've been hospitalized so many times, I've lost count. It's an hereditary condition that runs across both sides of my family. So, I had no chance of escaping. I thank God that I got it all under control thanks to my positive mindset, healthy attitude, excellent diet and my constant focus on health, wellness, exercise and great sleep.

If I was able to naturally kick one of The World Health Organization's official top 20 most debilitating health conditions on the Planet, – then my belief is that anything is possible for you too. (Punching my fist high in the air right now with joy, by the way).

---

*Exercise:*

*Think Positive - Your body reacts to your mood and state of mind. An unhappy person is more prone to fatigue and other illnesses.*

*What can you do to lead a positive lifestyle and be happy and content with who you are?*

---

www.MarieORiordanInternational.com

Nick James, Business Coach, Speaker, Internet Marketing Expert

# A Chance Meeting With An Entrepreneur, In A Car Park, In The Rain......

I was in my mid-twenties and living a drab, monotonous life with very little money, no prospects and a marriage that was going down the drain.

One day, while going through my usual lackluster routine of working as a car park attendant in Reading, Berkshire, I noticed that a beautiful 7 series, black BMW had been boxed into its parking space by a large white van.

It was teeming with rain, and when the BMW's owner returned and couldn't remove it, I invited him into my hut for a cup of tea whilst he waited for the owner of the van to return. I made some small talk and asked him what he did for a living – and how he had managed to become the owner of such a great car. He told me that he sold self-help tapes and gave me three of the VHS tapes to watch, asking me to give him a call if I was interested in taking these lessons further.

Well, the van driver came back and the businessman duly went on his way. I watched the tapes and was immediately inspired. I gave him a call and the rest, as they say, is history.

It just goes to show how opportunities can arise when you least expect them and that it's vitally important to recognize and value them when they do. Sometimes life gives you a break, but these opportunities must not be overlooked, because they just might give you the chance to change your life for the better.

www.Nick-James.com

Dr Jane Lewis, Career Coach

# Only Connect

*"Only connect! ... Connect the prose and the passion, and both will be exalted, and human love will be seen at its height. Live in fragments no longer. Only connect, and the beast and the monk, robbed of the isolation that is life to either, will die."*
E M Forster – Howard's End

We're all so busy running around doing, it's easy to lose our connection with ourselves, our environment and our friends and family. One of my Hawaiian teachers, when he travels to the Mainland, or to another country, always takes a moment when he gets off the 'plane to connect with the land around him. I've got into the habit of connecting with the world before I swing into action in the morning.

If you think we are not connected to the world around us, think again! Scientists like Bruce Lipton, a biologist by training, have shown that each and every cell is profoundly sensitive to its environment. Put very simply, proteins on the membrane that surrounds the cell act as switches that connect the cell with its environment. Individual cells can survive outside the body providing they are fed and watered correctly and given the right amount of light.

The cell's proteins give it information about what is going on in the environment, and then regulate the function and behavior of the cell in response to that information.

If that's what's going on at the level of every cell, then think how much more information there is when you combine those cells into a body. It all happens at a deeply unconscious level, and for many of us, that's where it stays. While things are going well, it's fine, but when things start to go wrong, we wonder what's going on.

When you start to connect, consciously at first, you increase your ability to tap into your own intuition and inner knowledge. It also helps you increase your focus and concentration to be in the moment. As my friend Dr Matt James of The Empowerment Partnership says, when you pause and bring everything into that moment, that's when you find the most empowerment: the power and *manna* to get through the day.

---

*Exercise:*

*When you wake up in the morning, take a moment to notice the world around you. Take a single breath in through your nose, and out through your mouth, and for that moment, connect. During the day, from time to time, take a moment just to stop and notice what you see/hear/smell/taste/feel.*

---

www.TheCareerSuccessDoctor.com

*"One new perception, one fresh thought,
one act of surrender,
one leap of faith
can change your life forever."*
Robert Holden

Emma Tiebens, Relational Marketer

# Choose Your Emotions

*"Do you CHOOSE to be happy or do you wait to FEEL happy?"*
Joyce Meyer

As an Author, Speaker and Online Marketing Consultant, I encounter a lot of people everyday offline and online. With all the uncertainties happening around us, it's inevitable that you will come across people who are disgruntled, frustrated, fearful and anxious. It only takes a teeny trigger and they blow up with an unexplainable reaction! These nasty negative emotions are so evident with people lately... unhappiness, hatred, rage...

I'm not saying we should never allow ourselves to feel negatively when we need to. All I am saying is that it is possible for us to have some control over our emotions by being aware of the state of our heart. For the past 2 years, I have gone through a roller coaster of emotions that is part of this long learning curve I chose to take on when I made a decision to transition from being an offline entrepreneur to how to become an effective online marketer.

When I would feel an onset of frustration and disappointment, my tendency was to wallow in it and have a 'pity party' for myself. Now I know that when I am feeling anxious and discouraged, what I need to do is transition from a place of ungratefulness to a place of gratitude, and I call that my 'pivot point'. That's when I ask myself:

**"Do I CHOOSE to be happy or do I wait to FEEL happy?"**

Ask yourself that question right now... what is your immediate answer?

---

*Exercise:*

*Make a list of what you're grateful for daily. Have a journal if you can't remember them. Memorize that list... have that become a part of your make-up. When you start feeling discouraged, review your list and it's amazing what that does!*

---

Gratitude is an attitude and it can be learned. What are you waiting for? Make your list now and start writing everything that you're grateful for now. You'll quickly realize that the glass was truly half full all along...you just thought it was half empty....

www.TheRelationalMarketer.com

*"Happiness is not in our circumstances but in ourselves. It is not something we see, like a rainbow, or feel, like the heat of a fire. Happiness is something we are."*
John B Sheerin

# Success Principle #4:
# Take Responsibility For Your Future

- Realize that you have freedom of choice and that, as such, you are completely responsible for your successes, your failures, your happiness and unhappiness. You are also responsible for your future.

- The opposite of accepting responsibility is making excuses and blaming people and things for what's going on in your life. Don't get into the habit of making excuses. Get into the habit of taking responsibility.

- Don't be afraid to ask for help if you need it, but remember the final decision is up to you.

- A basic law of human life (the Law of Causality) was first coined by Socrates more than 400 years BC. Nowadays, it is often called the Law of Cause and Effect. As Eve Grace-Kelly shows in her Life Lesson: *Are You At Cause Or At Effect?*, if you find yourself towards the At Cause end of the spectrum, you are likely to suffer from lack of enthusiasm, low motivation, stress, lack of fulfillment, etc.

- There is a direct link between responsibility, control, freedom and happiness. The more responsibility you take, the more in control you are. You will accept the freedom to make decisions and to do the things you want to do.

- Who in your life causes you stress or anxiety? Who is responsible for this cause? Are they responsible for being in your life, or are you responsible for having them in your life?

*"It's your life – embrace it, OWN it!"*
Vinden Grace

Eve Grace-Kelly, Success Coach, Author

# Are You At Cause Or Effect?

Once in a while, I need to take stock of whether I am at *cause* or at *effect* in my life. By this I mean, am I in control or am I purely reacting to whatever is happening around me. Primarily because, like so many other people, I often get swept along in life. Especially when we are so busy. I know I take on too much, and am always ready to say "Yes" before really assessing whether I can do something.

Bit by bit, the demands on us become so great, they become overwhelming. And, by the time we notice it, it's too late. We are no longer in control! We are no longer the creator of what happens, but are the victim of circumstances.

The problem with being 'at effect' is that we tend to look outside of ourselves for some cause that we can blame for what is happening. We'll always find a cause – but it may not be the real one. The real one is probably inside us.

As a child, I was probably always 'at effect'. But as I experienced life more, gained more confidence and spent time on my own personal development, I gradually swung more to the left – to the 'at cause' end of the spectrum - and started taking a firm hold of the reins of my own life.

*Exercise:*

*Ponder this:*

*Do things happen **TO** you? Or do things happen **BECAUSE** of you?*

*Where would you position yourself along the Cause and Effect Continuum?*

**Cause** **Effect**

*The following table gives some high level indicators on how to determine where you are. E.g. Choice vs. Excuses: do you embrace the ability to make choices in your life or do you find yourself making excuses as to why things do or don't happen?*

| At Cause | At Effect |
|---|---|
| Choice | Excuses |
| Action | Reaction |
| Responsibility | No responsibility |
| Position of power | Powerless/victim |

*The major roadblocks that stop us from moving more towards the At Cause end of the spectrum are:*

- *Procrastination*

- *Lack of enthusiasm*

- *Low motivation*

- *Fatigue*

- *Stress*

- *Lack of fulfilment*

- *Distractions*

*Do you recognize any of these in your life?*

Joe Kasper, Health Coach

# I Played God

My brother rang to say that my Dad, my hero, had had a massive stroke. He also said to bring a black suit, which meant that he thought my Dad would be dead sooner rather than later. I had one mission: to keep my Dad alive! I told my brother I would not bring a black suit. I knew that, somehow, my Dad would make it. When I arrived, Dad was in intensive care with tubes coming out of everywhere. I told friends and family at the hospital, "My Dad will make it, I guarantee it!" Someone said, "Joseph: who are you to play God?" I told her, "I JUST DID." At that point, I realized no-one was ever going to tell me what I can and cannot do again!

That same day our family physician told me that my Dad had, perhaps, 48 hours to live. I said, "You're wrong and you will be apologizing to me. He will make it!". Later in the day, my brother started telling Dad how great he is and that it's okay to let go. I said in a booming voice, "Fight, Fight. You will make it, Dad - never give up. We love you!" I called the school that I worked at and told them that my Dad was ill and that I would not be coming back. I made a decision to take over my Dad's healthcare, because I knew that is what my Dad would want.

Within a week, Dad's health started to improve, albeit a little. He was still unconscious, but he was breathing with the aid of a ventilator. A hospital doctor told me that Dad would probably be a vegetable for the rest of his life. I simply said, "Don't bet on it." A week later, he was moved out of intensive care, but still with a feeding tube and I was told that he would be completely paralyzed. That same day, my Dad opened his eyes. All of a sudden, after six weeks of no speech, he spoke, "Turn off the lights!" He was soon able to move his left arm and left leg, but the neurologist told me that his right side would be completely paralyzed. I replied "No way!" The neurologist said that a massive stroke causes brain damage and since Dad had been through so much, we shouldn't expect anything more. I told him, "You will eat those words. Tell me what cannot happen and I will make it happen."

I returned to the hospital the next day knowing that a breakthrough was about to happen. I asked the neurologist again, "What can you do to get my Dad to move his right leg?" To which he replied that he was sorry, but nothing more could be done. I asked the doctor to check my Dad's vital signs as I pulled up the blanket, grabbed the bottom of my Dad's foot and started to press on pressure points with major force. I put every ounce of my energy into Dad's right foot. I asked him to raise his left leg (the one that was functional), then to raise his right one (the paralyzed leg). He still could not move it. I was not leaving him until his right leg moved. I raised his right leg and then put my hands next to his foot, looking like I was raising it again. I said, "Dad, help me to raise your leg; we will do it together." As I carried out the motion with him, his leg raised up. I went back to applying acupressure to his right leg and his leg got higher and higher. My Dad had sent me a message that he was ready to make a remarkable recovery and I would be leading the charge.

I met with the hospital nutritionist who recommended a diet of hot dogs, chicken breast, and low-fat ice cream. I told her that from now on, I would handle his menu. I went to the hospital kitchen to make sure my Dad's meals were made as healthily as possible. I started to make juice from my machine at home and he drank it with his medicine.

My Dad started physical therapy in his room as he still could not walk. The therapist had to follow the hospital doctor's orders for therapy. I watched and realized that, once again, I would have to take over. A regime of 15 minutes basic range of motion on his right leg was not enough. I continued applying my manual physical therapy on my Dad, working with him daily for 30 minutes to 1 hour. I had one mission - to get him walking again; nothing was going to stop me. Within a few weeks, Dad was transferred to a nursing home. During my first visit there, I asked about the diet being fed to Dad and, once again, I was told that the nursing home was serving well-balanced meals: hot dogs, grilled cheese, and pudding. No wonder most people drop dead at these places. I told them that if they did not make an exception and prepare my Dad's food the way I wanted it, he was going to another facility. They agreed to work with me.

The next problem to contend with was DNR, which stands for Do Not Resuscitate, which was an order from the hospital. If the man can keep surviving, who are they to make this judgment? The nursing home wanted my Dad to make the decision for his own life. My brother did not want it. He was angry, but I knew my Dad would understand and agree with me. Picture me, my brother and a nursing home administrator asking my Dad what he should do if he had another life-threatening situation. He simply said, "I want to live!" Case closed!

My family and I ensured Dad had visitors every day he was at this nursing home. I bought food from a nearby health store to make sure he ate as much organic food as possible. Some months later, I received a call that my Dad would be coming home the next day as the doctor and physical therapist had decided that he was not going to progress any more. This meant time to go home and die. I made sure every day was a productive day for my Dad, which was filled with speech therapy, massage therapy, aqua therapy, physical therapy and chiropractic therapy. We also had a live-in attendant to be with him. My Mom worked full-time as a bank teller and I also had to find a job. I taught PE again, did bus duty, lunch duty, and personal training. Somehow, we were able to pay the bills for my Dad's care. He continued to improve. I told him every day how much I loved him and how proud I was of him. What I never told him was that the MRI of his brain showed 1/3 of his brain completely frayed from the stroke. He beat every obstacle thrown at him.

I had asked the president of my baseball league if my Dad could throw out the first pitch of a game when he walked again. Almost 1 year to the day of my Dad having a stroke, he was walking alone with a cane. Both teams were in tears. The league president handed him a baseball and he threw it to our catcher. My Dad had come full circle, and I realized how blessed I am to have such a role model.

I have said this time and time again; if I can be half the man Dad is, I am a lucky man.

Thank you for reading about my hero, Herbert Kasper.

His son, Joe Kasper

www.FireYourDiet.com

Vinden Grace, Internet Business Specialist/
Digital Coach

# Miscellaneous Life Lessons – Part II

Life lessons are not always those that people learn as a result of negative things that happen in their lives. There are also some fantastic life-affirming lessons to inspire us. Take, for example, Walt Disney's advice: *"Find a job that you like so much that you would do it without compensation; then do it so well that people will pay you to continue."*

Many of the contributors in this book do just that. They love what they do and also get so much out of helping others achieve success.

In addition to what our clients have sent to us, here are a couple of my own life lessons:

- Everyone is an example: choose to be a great one

- No matter what happens, look for the lesson

Do any the following resonate with you? Have you learned similar life lessons? Tick those that apply to you and work on integrating the lessons into your own life.

| I've learned that................ | ✓ |
| --- | --- |
| .... either you control your attitude or it controls you. | |
| .... sometimes when I'm angry I have the right to be angry, but that doesn't give me the right to be cruel. | |
| .... just because two people argue, it doesn't mean they don't love each other. And just because they don't argue, it doesn't mean they do love each other. | |
| .... we are responsible for what we do, no matter how we feel. | |
| .... there are people who love you dearly, but just don't know how to show it. | |
| .... true friendship continues to grow, even over the longest distance. The same goes for true love. | |

Kathleen Ronald, Networker, Speaker, Trainer, Consultant

# Keep Your Word!

Your words hold so much power, it is important to honor them. My father, Bob, a huge mentor in my life, ensured that I never forgot this lesson. I remember the day that, on the way home from work, due to traffic and weather conditions, I was an hour late for a scheduled call and he delivered a 45 minute lecture, emphasized with a colorful arrangement of words and emotions. I've never forgotten that wise and important lesson ~ **Keep your word**!

Why are these three simple little words so difficult for most people to honor or to own? Why do people have a hard time keeping their word? One reason, I think, is what I call the triple-AAA personality practice (deriving from the type A personality), which tends to over-commit. Another is the Mother Theresa syndrome: when people want to help everyone but haven't found the extra 48 hours a day to accommodate all those commitments. And then of course the 'mental-pause' crowd…we forget ~ nothing intentional…just happens. Those are but a few of the many possible reasons why folks can't keep their word.

There are countless benefits to Being your Word: People will like and trust you. You will have their respect and admiration. They will know they can count on you. If you don't keep your word, you get the opposite of those benefits. Wondering why your life isn't working out? **Keep your word!**

You may have mastered keeping your word to others, but keeping your word to yourself is critical and most people haven't even approached addressing that. Yet, your own self-respect depends on it! Your word is EVERYTHING! You will become a commodity when people can trust your word. Make this your personal and business brand. There isn't a marketing or sales product that can support the growth of your brand and business better than Being your word. I promise!

How to get started? The first step is most important – work to understand what prevents you from keeping your word. Then, address each issue with a solution. You can't afford not to 'get' this lesson today! You **must keep your word!**

---

*Exercise:*

*Where in your life are you **not** being your word? Practice being your word in that area until it is no longer an issue.*

*Make a list of agreements that you made but have yet to complete. One by one, complete each item on the list!*

*Before you verbalise any further agreements, be sure to check in with yourself to ensure you can follow through.*

---

www.Speaktacular.com

*"There are only two ways to live your life.*
*One is as though nothing is a miracle.*
*The other is as though everything is a miracle."*
Albert Einstein

Eve Grace-Kelly, Success Coach, Author

# Find The Right Balance For You

*"Real success is finding your lifework in the work that you love."*
David McCullough

As a certified Work-Life Balance Coach, I often have to stop and ask myself: am I walking the talk? I know the theories of getting that precarious balance between work and your non-work life in balance; I coach people on how to achieve Work-Life Balance; I've even lectured on the subject internationally on several occasions! However, like doctors who smoke and drink excessively or cobbler's children having no or bad shoes, it doesn't always mean that I follow my own advice!

Being something of a sunshine freak, I do take the opportunity when there's a spot of sun to pop into the garden with my personal development reading and note-taking. I often go walking in those 'wobbly' trainers that are said to improve your posture and work your leg muscles more (they certainly do the latter!)..... It gives the locals a giggle as I totter around the cobbled streets!

The challenge for me is balancing my ambition to help lots of people through coaching, coupled with a desire to travel and experience living in a number of foreign countries, plus aiming to work part-time to spend more time on non-business activities – all of which means it's a really difficult balance to get right.

Another issue in terms of Work-Life Balance is that I'm blessed in that I really enjoy my work! This means that I'm reluctant to stop working.... But I find that when I do, I get fresh energy and ideas to feed into my coaching work as I'm gaining exposure to other areas, so I know it's both good for me and for the business and hence our clients.

I believe that Work-Life Balance is different for everyone. For some, they need to work 9-5 and have completely different interests outside their perhaps mundane work. Others, like scientists, live and breathe their work. I fall pretty close to being in the latter camp, but I do have hobbies or interests I'd like to pursue. I'd love to learn to play the piano and how to draw and paint. The balance between work and life changes over time as well. And, it's a good idea to look at this every few months or so, especially if you have a busy life or if there is one particular focus at the moment. I've recently gone through this re-balancing exercise myself and have re-structured my business in a way that I now have more freedom to pursue other interests. The focus hasn't gone from the business itself, only the way I do things now. With our various membership sites, I can write an article once and many people will benefit from it, as opposed to exclusively helping one person at a time, or a few in a group session, in our coaching business. The latter methods are fulfilling but slow going in terms of making an impact on lots of people.

I get most fulfillment by coaching clients one-to-one. However, that means that I can't help as many people as I feel I'm here to do. It also means that I'm working very long hours and can't pursue my other interests. So, I've found ways to reduce my working time, but increase my revenues through joint ventures, automation and delegation. Finally, I've listened to my own Work-Life Balance training!

---

*Exercise:*

*Imagine that you feel in balance with everything in your world; that both your personal and work lives are in perfect harmony.*

*Write down what this feels like. Where are you? Who are you with? What are you doing? What do you see around you? What does your ideal working week look like? Do you work from home or do you go to a place of work? How long a journey do you have? How much leisure time do you have? Who do you spend it with?*

*Now compare this ideal balance with what you currently have.*

*What needs to change to move towards a better work-life balance for you?*

*When are you going to take that first step?...............*

---

www.QCCGroup.com

Vinden Grace, Internet Business Specialist/ Digital Coach

# Your Skill May Be Another's Challenge

When my dad was in his early 80s, he expressed an interest in computing. He wanted to do some web-browsing to check out golf courses (he's a golfing fanatic and still plays twice a week at the age of 87!), plus research his family history, and write his life story, together with keeping in email contact with me wherever our travels are constantly taking us. So we gave him a computer to kick-start the process.

I had been a Project Manager for a global training company, plus Dad was in a technical division of the Army during the Second World War, so I assumed that it would not be a major challenge to teach him how to use a computer. What I had overestimated was his exposure to using recent technology (he doesn't even use ATMs), so it presented more of a challenge than I had anticipated. Dad did OK, but I would approach it differently now.

I gleaned two lessons from this experience: firstly, that I had made an assumption about an older generation's exposure to technology in general, assuming that, because it's all around them, they would be familiar with it. Not so! This meant that I should have taken a different approach to teaching Dad. Many of us forget that we've been exposed from a young age to more and more technology as we've gone through life. I first used a computer in 1973! Our mobile phones are now PDAs (Personal Digital Assistants or mini-computers), with so much more computing power than the paper-tape-reading computer

I started on. So, for people of my dad's generation, even technically savvy ones like him, the learning curve with computing is much steeper than for many of us, something I certainly needed to take into account when teaching him.

Secondly, he's a quick learner who is mentally and physically very fit, so if he struggled a bit early on, it shows what challenges others of that generation also face day-to-day in using modern technology, the familiarity with and use of which many of us take for granted. We could all do with being patient when older people are struggling with technology. Let's all remember that the next time a retired person is holding up the queue at the post office or bank when using the ATM, etc…

Resources: www.SilverSurfersComputerTraining.com (for the over 50s) or www.OnlineTrainingInComputerSkills.com (for anyone who's not a complete beginner) or www.BeginnersComputerTraining.com (for anyone new to computing).

*"If the past cannot teach the present and the father cannot teach the son, then history need not have bothered to go on, and the world has wasted a great deal of time."*
Russell Hoban

Caroline Marsh, Property Investor

# Developing An Attitude And Mindset Of How To Change When Things Change

I only have to look at my life to see that the only constant is change.

I learnt very quickly to adapt to change, even coming to the UK from Zambia was a challenge; the system is different, people are different, work ethics are also different. And, as if that's not enough, the weather is very, very different! But I had to face my fears and do it anyway.

In 2008, part of my business goal was to buy six more properties. Suddenly, planning legislation changed and so did my focus. I then found myself bogged down with why they had changed legislation and spent half of my time in meetings every other day with officers, not making any progress. I felt so frustrated and I didn't understand their logic, because we were meeting the housing shortage and they were almost clamping us down. It took me six months to realize that I was going nowhere with my attitude and by then, the property market had changed and we were affected by the bank's Loan To Value (LTV). Mortgages went from 90% LTV to 75%; I felt as if the whole business world was collapsing on me. Things were changing rapidly and I did not want them to change.

I later had a meeting with my business partner who asked me a very good question: *"Caroline, the market has changed. What will you do next?"* We had a strategic meeting and found solutions - I ended up buying only two properties, which was very disappointing for me.

My biggest lesson was learning how to respond when things change. I have now developed a mindset and an attitude of how to change when things change. Besides the bible, Seth Godin's book *The Dip* and *Who Moved My Cheese?* by Spencer Johnson, were the greatest books that helped me.

www.CarolineMarsh.com

# Success Principle #5:
# Grow Your Social Capital –
# Go The Extra Mile

- Success is social. It contains all the ingredients of success that we customarily think of as individual – talent, intelligence, education, effort and luck, but it is also greatly intertwined with networks.

- Think of it as social capital. Where financial capital is the accumulation of material wealth, e.g. money or property, social capital is the accumulation of resources developed during the course of connecting with people, especially through personal and professional networks. Resources include opportunities, contacts, information, ideas, knowledge, and, of course, referrals. They also include things like trust, confidence, friendship, good deeds and goodwill.

- There is a saying: 'What goes around, comes around'. If you give more and give a better service than you are paid for, eventually you will get huge returns from your investment (not just monetary, but from deeper, more fulfilling relationships). As Bev James states in her Life Lesson: **True Value Doesn't Always Come From Putting A Price Tag On Everything You Do**: *"My philosophy is always to give before you get when building a new business relationship. Giving makes you feel good and will make your associates feel valued and appreciated. It may be something simple like a business contact; it could be something greater like a discount or a complementary product or service. Giving before you get and putting aside the price tag, helps to create a climate of good will – in which loyalty develops and even better things will happen."*

- Always think in terms of what you can do for the other person.

- Be kind and generous to all; you never know where your breakthrough will come from.

Mindy Gibbins-Klein, Speaker, Author, Publisher

# Stop Being So Hard On Yourself

Imagine if your best friend started criticizing you in public. Not only telling you what you are doing badly, but exaggerating things and in a loud voice too. You might be angry and upset, and quite possibly embarrassed. It might make you start to wonder about the value you provide. Either way, you wouldn't put up with it for long. You expect a friend to be there for you, to boost you up and remind you how great you are. You would either let that friend know their outburst was unacceptable, or you would end the friendship.

The sad thing is that many people do let this kind of criticism go on too long, and they can't get rid of the person because they are the culprits. They are their own harshest critics. Have you ever caught yourself in the middle of a self-deprecating rant? The kind that is going nowhere but down? I believe that it doesn't matter what happens in your life, or how others treat you. You can still be your own best friend: encouraging, positive and supportive. In fact, I think you absolutely need to develop that kind of self-encouragement, to achieve great things.

In ten years of helping people write and publish books, I have probably seen and heard more than my fair share of people beating themselves up. There is something about writing a book, which brings out the most destructive self-doubt and anxiety. Of all the fears people experience, the strongest and most dangerous one is the fear that they do not add value, or worse, that their ideas will be ridiculed. If left unchecked, the little voice may start to erode the aspiring author's sense of self-confidence. *"Who am I to try to write a book? What do I have to say anyway? Why would anyone listen to me?"*

Luckily, we have helped lots of people get over that and experience the joy of holding their book in their hands, and sharing their message with others. I often use other metaphors in my speaking, since not everyone wants to write a book. Training for a marathon, starting a new business or getting divorced can bring up similar fears. Fear is normal. But personal insults are not – especially when you attack yourself.

The best way to deal with lack of self-confidence is to overpower it with something positive. Start with the big reason why. Many motivational speakers have said that if the 'why' is big enough, the 'how' doesn't matter. It's true! Think about something you did that was out of your comfort zone, challenging or even downright scary! If you achieved it in the end, despite your fears, you must have really wanted it.

You also need to have a higher purpose. My most successful clients have found it a breeze to write books and do other challenging things, when they were thinking of others. Who will benefit? How many people can you help? This focus on others makes it next to impossible to think about your own little doubts. You simply can't focus on both at the same time.

Good luck with this practice. It is very worthwhile, in the pursuit of everything that is most important to you. And who knows, you may even gain a new best friend – you!

www.BookMidwife.com

www.Ecademy-Press.com

*"The chief cause of failure and unhappiness is trading what we want most for what we want at the moment."*
Author Unknown

Dr William Davey, Former Physician to HM
Queen Elizabeth II

# Listen With Intent

*"It is the disease of not listening, the malady of not marking,
that I am troubled withal."*
William Shakespeare

*"People talking without speaking;
People hearing without listening......."*
Paul Simon (songwriter)

Over a lifetime as a doctor helping people with their problems, and aware of my own mistakes made in private relationships, I have so often thought that the art of listening, with sincerity and sensitivity, is fundamental to the success or failure in personal liaisons. This is also true in the social and international sphere. However, my concern here is to briefly consider listening in the intimate interpersonal situation.

Sweeping statements are always too general; however based upon my experience, I have to say that not all men are good at listening to their girlfriend, partner or spouse. So often, men hear without properly listening.

Men, imagine this role-play. You have arrived home tired after a hard day at work and you sit down for a meal with the lady in your life who, after her own long day, particularly wants to talk. Do you listen, really listen? (The roles are interchangeable of course and, equally apply to, same sex relationships.)

In my experience, I have learned that women in general need to talk far more than men do and they really need to be listened to properly by the loved one in their life. I have also learned that women are not necessarily seeking answers to the questions that might arise from what they are saying. When I first realized this, it came as a humbling surprise.

My personal discovery was that, so frequently, all a woman needs is to be listened to with sensitivity, sincerity and understanding. It almost seems hardwired into a man, or at least in my case, to respond immediately with a solution or quick fix to all that has been said. This accentuates the importance of listening properly to what is being said and not rushing to a conclusion.

It is also important to listen to the silences as well, which involves looking at the person who has been speaking, making eye contact, and watching facial expressions. As you love your partner, you will be well accustomed to their eyes and their mouth.   These both express so often the depths of her soul without the use of words.

So listening is not just attending to the words uttered but looking with care at the face and engaging properly with the person opposite you with genuine concern and attentiveness.

It is also important to think clearly, as to what has been left unsaid and consider the implications. This may require asking for clarification, but do this with sensitivity.

So many mistakes are made by assuming that you have fully understood what has been said to you.

If you are tired, if you are on edge, if there is an atmosphere, then in my experience it is almost certainly true that even if you have listened with the greatest care, you may have misunderstood something and received an impression that is **different from what has been intended**. Explaining what you have perceived as you have listened can clarify so much that can be unnecessarily misunderstood or even resented.

Sometimes it is not even needful to have understood completely what has been said. I have learned that the very act of listening is very reassuring and a very helpful experience for the speaker. It is also one of the greatest sources of bonding between two people. It shows how much you value your partner.

Very importantly, listening is something that relieves stress, acting as a safety valve, causing harmony to return where there was unhappiness, bringing healing in a multitude of ways

I have no doubt that listening properly to your loved one should become an automatic part of your lifestyle, if it is not already.

It is something never to be neglected and needs constant daily attention. It will ensure happiness in your relationship and enhance the possibility of it enduring into the future.

*Exercise:*

*Simply ask yourself.....*

- *Do you really listen to your partner?*

- *Do you interrupt when your partner is speaking and so cause frustration by your premature interjections?*

- *Do you seek for clarification or just assume that you have heard and understood?*

- *Have you experienced what 'good listening' does for the harmony of your relationship?*

www.GeneLifestyle.com

*"Find a quiet place and listen. It should be very quiet. The only sound you should hear is your heart beating. Listen. Peer deep down inside your heart. Do you see someone that holds a special place in your heart? Maybe they have always been there when you needed them; maybe they offered words of encouragement; taught you a lesson; comforted you when you were sick; praised you on your accomplishments. Make this their lucky day. You have the POWER to spread happiness today. A quick note or a kind word is all it takes to bring a smile and lasting memory to someone very special."*

Gary Harrington

Eve Grace-Kelly, Success Coach, Author

# Nurture The Right Thoughts

The following is a Cherokee story that has been around for a long time.

One evening, an elderly Cherokee told his grandson about a battle that goes on inside people.

He said, *"My son, the battle is between two wolves inside us all.*

*One wolf is Evil. It is anger, envy, jealousy, sorrow, regret, greed, arrogance, self-pity, guilt, resentment, inferiority, lies, false pride, superiority, and ego.*

*The other one is Good. It is joy, peace, love, hope, serenity, humility, kindness, benevolence, empathy, generosity, truth, compassion and faith."*

The grandson thought about it for a minute and then asked his grandfather: *"Which wolf wins?"*

The old Cherokee simply replied, *"The one you feed"*.

The essence of the story is about nurturing the right thoughts. The reason I love this story is because we can apply it in so many other ways.

For example, the Evil wolf could be called 'Limiting Belief' and the Good wolf could be called 'Empowering Belief'. Or 'Can Do' and 'Can't Do'. Or 'Uncertainty' and 'Self-assurance'.

---

*Exercise:*

*What are your wolves called?*

*Which wolf are you choosing to feed right now?*

*Is it the right one to feed?*

*It doesn't really matter what we call them. The key thing is that we have a choice in which one we feed.*

---

www.QCCGroup.com

Gurbaksh Chahal, Entrepreneur

# Living The Dream

*"Everything starts with a dream, a particle of our imagination
that teases us of what the future could be like,
as long as we fight for it......"*
Gurbaksh Chahal

I encourage people to effectively harness risk and discipline for their own gain. I do this by sharing my personal vision and experiences – success is much closer than many aspiring entrepreneurs realize!

In my book, *The Dream*, I talk about my journey and about the lessons I have learned. Some of the key ones are here – one for each year of my life!

1)  Always surround yourself with people who want you to succeed. That seems simple on the surface, but when you get out there, in the real world, you will discover that most people are rooting for you to fail. STAY AWAY FROM THEM!

2)  Never do anything for money – or, at least, solely for money. Of course, you want to make money, but if that's the only goal, it will adversely affect all of your decisions. They will be colored by greed. SO DON'T LET MONEY DEFINE THE BEGINNING OF THE JOURNEY; MAKE MONEY THE RAINBOW THAT COMES AT THE END.

3)  If you genuinely want something, don't wait for it – teach yourself to be impatient. PATIENCE MAY WELL BE A VIRTUE, BUT IMPATIENCE HAS ALWAYS WORKED BETTER FOR PEOPLE.

4)  The biggest lessons come from the biggest mistakes. Never put yourself in a position of vulnerability. ALWAYS OWN YOUR MISTAKES.

5)  Don't chase the money. Chase substance. If you have substance, the MONEY WILL FOLLOW.

6) FIX A THING BEFORE IT BREAKS, rather than don't fix it if it's not broken.

7) DON'T BE JEALOUS. Jealousy is one of the most useless emotions on the planet.

8) Some people are like crabs. If they can't get over the wall, they will PULL YOU DOWN TO KEEP YOU FROM CLIMBING OVER.

9) Most people think that they need to know exactly what they want to do when they start a business, but they're wrong. If you go into something with a very specific plan, you might be so focused on your goal that you would not see the PROMISING OPPORTUNITIES that present themselves as you make your way along.

10) Failure is not an option. Anyone who even entertains the idea of failure is already doomed. Whenever you set out to do something, large or small, you have to believe in your heart that it's going to happen, and you have to keep moving toward the goal.

11) Learn to move on when it's time to move on. Bite the bullet. Let go. START AFRESH. Don't look back. It's not as easy as it sounds, but make the effort – it's worth it.

12) DON'T LOSE YOUR MORAL BAROMETER. Lies and obfuscation might give you short-term success, but they make for very unstable relationships. Never compromise your morality. We all need to live by a moral code.

13) CRITICISM is the best form of discipline because it makes you look at yourself.

14) LISTEN TO YOUR HEART. We tend to do well at things we love, so find something you love – or learn to love what you're doing.

15) ADJUST YOUR ATTITUDE. Without the right attitude, you'll never succeed. You have to believe in yourself, often to the point of madness, because until you prove yourself, the only people who believe in you are your parents. If you have any doubts, get out now.

16) FIGURE OUT WHAT YOU'RE GOOD AT. Very few of us are gifted, so we need to work with the gifts we have. If you're five-foot-two and you love basketball, let me be the first to tell you, it's probably not going to happen! (But don't let me to stop you.)

17) TRUST YOUR GUT. We are complicated creatures. That inexplicable feeling you get sometimes – well, it tends to be right a lot more often than it's wrong. Try not to overanalyze it. Some

mysterious inner you is trying to help by pointing you in the right direction.

18) DO YOUR HOMEWORK. BEFORE YOU START ANYTHING. Make sure you know exactly what you're getting into. Ignorance is dangerous. What you don't know can and will hurt you.

19) DON'T EXPECT PERFECTION from yourself or others, but never stop striving for it, and try to inspire others to strive for it too.

20) LEARN TO LISTEN. Everyone has an opinion, and everyone is entitled to an opinion, and even wrong-headed opinions can open your eyes to things you might otherwise have missed. So listen, even to people you disagree with – and maybe to them more than others. Then process what you've heard and have the courage of your convictions.

21) Own your mistakes. At the end of the day, every decision you make, even if it was inspired by misguided advice, is your decision. NOBODY WINS WHEN YOU START LOOKING FOR SOMEONE TO BLAME. Let it go. Keep moving. Forward movement is everything.

22) DON'T PROCRASTINATE . Procrastination is just another word for wanting to fail. If you're not hungry enough; if you're too lazy to move forward, you're never going to get anywhere.

23) EXPECT THE UNEXPECTED. If you're ready for anything, you'll still be unpleasantly surprised – but at least you'll get through it.

24) BE FEARLESS. The road to success is paved with failures. If you're afraid to fail, you'll never succeed.

25) Grow a thick skin – a very thick skin. People will question your ability to succeed and the loudest among them might make you doubt your own talents, so you'll need a thick skin to drown out the noise. THE SILENCE WILL HELP YOU FOCUS ON YOUR OBJECTIVE, AND YOU WILL PREVAIL.

26) TAKE CHANCES. Without risk, there is no reward. But make sure it's intelligent risk. Only a fool bets against Tiger Woods (until it is time to bet against Tiger Woods).

27) When you commit, you really have to commit. BECOME UNSTOPPABLE AND DON'T QUIT.

28) SUCCESS IS REALLY ABOUT MAKING IT HAPPEN. It's about dreaming. It's about finding that one thing you love above all others and then figuring out how to do it better than anyone else.

John Purkiss, Executive Headhunter

# The Power Of Acceptance

For me, one of the biggest life lessons is ***acceptance***. Once I understood this and began to put it into practice, everything changed for the better.

Acceptance means accepting the universe as it is. You accept the situation as it is. You accept other people as they are. You accept yourself as you are, including your body, your mind and any abilities you may or may not have been given. You also accept your thoughts and emotions as they arise.

Acceptance has many advantages. You no longer waste energy on judging people or situations, or dreaming about some time in the past or the future when things were or might be different. You are here, now – poised to take action.

Acceptance does not mean you do not care about other people or what is going on in the world. It means you accept your starting point. If your mind is clear and free from judgments, you can take the right action at the right time. If a child or a dog runs out into the road, you can intervene immediately. Accepting yourself and other people will transform your relationships. It can also have a big, positive effect on your career and your finances. Another word for acceptance is love.

I learned about acceptance shortly before my father died, after he had suffered from multiple sclerosis for many years. I accepted that he was dying and that all I could do was be with him and the rest of my family. After his death, I grieved in the normal way. However, I knew my destination, which was acceptance. We also found a way to celebrate his life, by publishing a book of his photographs.

Once you accept things as they are, you can spend a few minutes each day visualizing the way you want them to be. Then you take action steadily in your intended direction, allowing things to fall into place naturally.

How can we learn to accept? I find meditation helps a lot. When the mind is still, there are few, if any, thoughts. Many of us experience *pure consciousness*. You *are*, but there are no thoughts. Pure consciousness exists in all of us. Once you start to see yourself in other people, it becomes much easier to accept them as they are.

The above text is an extract from my fifth book. You can download the introduction to this, free of charge, at www.JohnPurkiss.com.

---

*Exercise:*

*As you carry out your normal activities throughout the day, observe what goes on around you.  This includes the way people speak and behave, the weather, the pace at which things happen or don't happen, the thoughts that enter your mind, and so on.*

*The thoughts may include judgments such as, "she shouldn't have said that", "people shouldn't do that", "what a stupid situation" and so on. Instead of clinging to them, you can just let them go.  It is important not to resist them, since it makes it harder to let go of them.  The judgments are largely involuntary and are not 'yours' in the first place.*

*Imagine you are standing on a bridge, looking down into a river in full flood. All kinds of thoughts – including judgments – rush down the river towards you. However, you can just watch them flow by beneath you. Fairly soon these judgments will vanish, and new thoughts may appear.  You can let them go too.*

*Now you can do what needs to be done at the appropriate time.*

---

www.JohnPurkiss.com

Glenn Harrold, Hypnotherapist

# Anything Is Possible...

*Always believe that anything is possible.*

I began producing my first hypnosis recordings around 12 years ago, from a box-room in my tiny two-bed terraced house. I used to meditate every day, focusing on manifestation so that they would sell in big numbers. Today, my tapes and CDs have sold well over a million copies.

Repeat the following affirmations – they can be repeated silently or out loud.

**"I am always in the right place at the right time"**

**"I draw opportunities towards me"**

www.HypnosisAudio.com

*"Don't say you don't have enough time. You have exactly the same number of hours per day that were given to Helen Keller, Michelangelo, Mother Teresa, Leonardo da Vinci, Thomas Jefferson, and Albert Einstein."*
H. Jackson Brown

# Success Principle #6:
# Start SMART… Get SMARTER

- Once you know what you want to achieve or become, you need to define it by making it a goal.

- As Jane Lewis says is her Life Lesson: **Make Your Goals SMART Ones**, your goal has to be SMART (Specific, Measurable, Attainable and Attractive, Realistic (no point setting an unrealistic goal such as "I want to be a millionaire by this evening") and Time-bound).

- Goals should have a WOW! Factor, so now make your goal even SMART**ER** by giving it some **E**motional **R**esonance.

- Think about how you feel in relation to the goal.  How committed are you to achieving it (see Success Principle #8)?  Is the goal a chore or something that really resonates with you?  How are you going to feel when you succeed? What will that give you?

- Ensure your success by:

  1. Writing your goal down on paper and keeping it somewhere where you can refer to it every day.

  2. Visualizing what it is going to feel and look like when you succeed.

  3. Keeping track of how you are progressing.

  4. Getting a support network going.  Tell a few people who you trust and know will support you.

*"By recording your dreams and goals on paper, you set in motion the process of becoming the person you most want to be."*
Mark Victor Hansen

Penny Power, Founder of Ecademy.com, Social Networking Expert, Author

# Staying Power

In a world where we are constantly being shown the next great thing and the next brilliant idea, there is a pressure on everyone to follow the crowd and keep adapting themselves and their businesses. When I meet and mentor business start-ups and established businesses that want to run faster, one of the things I say to them is *"drop your shoulders, take a big breath and come down to basics"*. The reason I say this is because people are getting caught up in technology hype, forgetting that, ultimately, the best thing for business is to 'connect, listen and talk'.

I recently had a wonderful morning with a colleague, Tom Evans. He was helping me plan some ideas into my upcoming workshop for Ecademy members. We were structuring the workshop on the principle of being Known, Liked and Followed.

Within the workshop, were some exercises on, 'What do you want to be known for?', 'Why do people like and trust you?' and, ultimately, 'What are you leading so that others can follow?'.

Tom and I asked each other what we liked about one another. I said that I liked him as he gave 'comfort' when I am with him. He was quite moved by that. Tom said to me that he liked me because I had 'Staying Power'.

I have thought a great deal about this since. Thank you, Tom. I guess that, in a mad world, one constant that Ecademy has given is that we are always there, safe, strong and supportive. Glenn, Thomas and I do have 'Staying Power'. We have remained independent and personally very committed to the journey of our members for over 12 years.

I once read this paragraph in a magazine - an interview with Edwin Moses, the American 400-meter hurdler who had an unbroken run of 122 victories over 9 years, nine months and nine days:

*"I certainly worked harder than everyone else, but I definitely wasn't any more talented. My high school was very strong in track and field events and there were a lot of students who were better than me. But I didn't mind training hard and working myself to improve. I was more determined and stuck at it more than other guys who were better than me, but who lost the necessary drive somewhere along the line. It never entered my mind that I was something special, that I had a talent or anything like that. I made it to the top of track and field, but I might equally have done so in physics or another area of science instead. That's the way I was raised."*

(Courtesy of Mercedes® magazine)

So I dedicate this life lesson to all the small businesses working hard across the globe; to everyone who has tenacity and drive and who works so hard and never gives up.

Find the thing you love and then stick at it.

---

*Exercise:*

*What do you love doing and what gives you 'Staying Power'?*

*How can you use this 'Staying Power' in other areas of your life?*

---

www.Ecademy.com

John Lees, Career Strategist

# Being Happy Is Serious Stuff

*"If you only ever live half your life,
the other half will haunt you forever."*

I wish I knew the author of those words. I heard them from a motivational speaker who once served as an air force pilot, speaking in San Francisco in the mid-80s. It's a good reminder of the powerful effect of our 'unlived lives', as Carl Jung described them. Jung suggested that our unlived lives have a huge effect not only on ourselves but also on our children. I wonder how many of us live merely haunted by what could have been?

I am an unrestrained believer in the importance of happiness. People misunderstand the idea and believe it's the same thing as satisfaction. Passing experiences or moments of indulgence bring satisfaction, which, although a welcome distraction, is nearly always temporary. Happiness is something deeper – it changes you, allows you to be at peace with yourself and useful to others – signs of a life well lived, you might say.

As a career coach, I naturally focus on how happy people are at work. Surveys suggest that up to three out of four people are unhappy in the work they do. Even more worrying, many don't believe that they could or should be happy at work. We need to take work satisfaction seriously, simply because we spend more hours in work than previous generations. Between the age of 18 and 60, most of the hours where you are energized and focused will be used up in work-related activity. Work creates a huge slice of your self-esteem, learning, security and social connection - for most adults, the job you choose to do is the most important life decision after choice of partner.

For too long, we've allowed happiness to be a fluffy concept owned by therapists and disconnected from the cut and thrust of work. We recognize that external factors (money, security, status) are far less likely to make us happy at work, and that something deeper is required. People talk about activity that is worthwhile, meaningful, 'putting something back'. You may be tempted by the fantasy that something undiscovered out there might be the right thing, but you place it at arm's length by calling it a 'dream job'. To do so is a perfect career strategy, because you don't have to do anything about it.

Taking happiness seriously only requires small steps. I find that people are happy in work when there is a 70% overlap between their role and what they find fulfilling. People who start to live their unlived lives don't have great career planning genes, but begin by doing two things. They match personal goals with the real needs and aspirations of employers, and negotiate a job-shaped overlap. And they talk to people to find out what's out there, and keep on asking, "who else should I be talking to?".

Living a complete life may be a kind of *vocation* - a word used so widely that we forget that a genuine calling isn't just about you and me. Happiness isn't about what we draw out from life; it's about finding the thing that helps us to engage, to participate, to give something to others. And if you find what you're looking for – pass it on.

Which takes me to a life lesson of even greater value, words from a gospel written by Matthew, a loan shark transformed by a rather special Galilean.

*"The kingdom of heaven is like treasure hidden in a field, which someone found and hid; then in his joy he goes and sells all that he has and buys that field."*

www.JohnLeesCareers.com

Eve Grace-Kelly, Success Coach, Author

# Give Priority To The Right Things

During my school years, I was quite studious and therefore quite shocked when a teacher entered the class on the first day of term and said to the whole class, *"Most of you will fail this class, not because you're not smart or won't work hard, but because of time management."* We all thought he'd got out of the wrong side of bed that morning, and that he wanted to scare us into working harder!

I didn't really think any more about it until towards the end of the school year – exams were looming and that's when I realized what he meant and that he was serious about it. Not because I didn't work hard – I did. But even though we had a year planner for our work, very few of us in the class really did any strategic thinking about how we were going to get through the mountain of work and studying that was needed. Bit by bit, week by week, month by month, my study milestone goals slipped. Back then, I had totally underestimated the importance of time management and setting up goals strategically. This was my first and most critical lesson in time management. One that I never forgot.

This lesson served me well early on in my career as a Project Manager and has had a profound effect on my life. As I'm sure you've found out, there are many, many books and articles around on time management. But one story that I relate to my coaching clients with time management issues is this:

*One day, an old professor was invited to lecture on the topic of 'Efficient Time Management' in front of a group of executive managers representing the largest, most successful companies in America. Standing in front of this group of elite managers, the professor slowly met eyes with each manager, one by one, and finally said, "We are going to conduct an experiment".*

*From under a table, the professor pulled out a big glass jar and gently placed it in front of him. Next, he pulled out a bag of stones, each the* size of a tennis ball, and placed them one by one in the jar. He did this until there was no room to add another stone in the jar.

The professor then asked the managers, "Is the jar full?" The managers replied, "Yes". The professor paused for a moment, and replied, "Really?" Once again, he reached under the table and pulled out a bag full of pebbles and carefully poured the pebbles into the jar, slightly rattling the jar allowing the pebbles to slip through the larger stones, until they settled at the bottom.

Again, the professor asked his audience, "Is the jar full now?" At this point, the managers began to understand his intentions.

One replied, "Apparently not!" "Correct", replied the old professor, who proceeded to pull out a bag of sand from under the table, and poured it into the jar, filling the spaces between the stones and the pebbles. Yet again, the professor asked, "Is the jar full?" Unanimously, the entire audience shouted "NO!" "Correct", replied the professor.

The professor reached for the pitcher of water that was on the table, and poured water in the jar until it was full.

The professor then asked the managers, "What great truth can we surmise from this experiment?" One manager quickly replied, "We learn that, as full as our schedules may appear, if we only increase our effort, it is always possible to add more meetings and tasks."

"No", replied the professor. "The great truth from this experiment is that, if we don't put all the larger stones in the jar first, we will never be able to fit all of them in later."

This story is all about identifying what the large stones are – the important things in our life or the high priority stuff – and making sure that we have time for these.

If we don't include the large stones in our life, we are likely to miss out on so much. If we give more priority to the small things in life, i.e. the pebbles and sand, our lives will be filled with less important things, leaving very little time for the really important things in our lives.

---

Exercise:

Make a list of your large stones. Is it your family? Your health? Your goals? Your career? Taking time out for yourself?

Then make a list of your pebbles; then your sand..... you get the idea.

Use these lists to resolve conflicts in prioritising things in your life.

---

Kathleen Ronald, Networker, Speaker, Trainer, Consultant

# ADD The Exclamation Mark (!) To YOUR Life!

I discovered through Google that the exclamation mark (!) is said to have originally been the Latin word for Joy, *Io*, with the I written above the o. Who knew? What an exciting thought! I don't know about you but I spent most of my adult life wondering what my purpose was in the world. I spent years contemplating this thought, until one of my spiritual teachers shared with me this thought:

*"My dear Kathleen; it is your birthright to be IN JOY! As you've spent years trying to identify your big purpose you've missed the most important part of living ~ if you are in JOY then, my dear one, YOU are on purpose!"*

She was so right. What a miracle concept ~ We are on purpose if we are in JOY! Purpose is not something that we need to chase or discover in life, but to live your exclamation mark! Your joy is the true indicator and compass for knowing that you are living on purpose. So many people wait for something to happen rather than 'creating' their lives and launching their dreams. A life that is short on joy's exclamation marks is a life without self-expression and one that is heading for sadness, regret, and disappointment. Just imagine your life if everything you did, all of your daily activities, were sprinkles of joy-full Exclamation Marks!!!

*Make a Mark!*

*Make a Positive Statement!*

*Make a life that is full of surprises!*

*Create Excitement!*

*Make a Difference in your world!*

*Be an Inspiration to those around you!*

*Exercise:*

*Focus on only doing the things that bring you JOY! Consider that any task regardless can be joyful if you choose to find the JOY in the action.*

*Have you put your goals on hold? Whether it's to write a book, discover a new destination, learn a new language or run a marathon ~ DO IT NOW! Ask yourself, "Have I added my joy MARK on my life?" Brainstorm often, asking, "How can I add the !!! to all that I do?".*

*Why do you put off your joy in favor of glum duty? Why don't you follow the 'get to' path instead of the 'have to'? Are there activities in your life that can become exclamation marks simply by reframing, by remembering they contain your joy? Let's make this tiny mark be a BIG lesson for our life. Only do what brings you JOY! It is as easy as adding the (!) mark! What are YOU waiting for?*

www.Speaktacular.com

*"The minute you settle for less than you deserve, you get even less than you settled for."*
Maureen Dowd

Seema Sharma, Dentist, Entrepreneur, Philanthropist

# Assess Your Priorities In Life

At the age of 35, I was juggling a career in dentistry, two daughters under the age of five, a husband with a meteoric career in cardiology and a newfound interest in property development. By 2007, as I turned 40, my property portfolio was successful and I suddenly realized that I could take a step back and decide to explore new territories.

After renovating two period homes and investing in commercial and residential property, my passion for property and architecture was still rivaled by my love for my career in dentistry, even though 80% of my financial success had come from 20% of my efforts.

At 40, with daughters aged just 10 and 8, and a dependable dream team akin to my second family, I cut back my hours at work and participated in a children's oral health education project in East London to pursue my dream to help those who had not been as fortunate.

That dream came true two years later, in 2009, when I was part of a winning team that secured a coveted tender to run an NHS dental practice for underprivileged residents in Bow, and I was invited to India to be the 'real Slumdog Secret Millionaire' in the popular Channel 4 philanthropy series.

---

*Exercise:*

*Is your life full of tasks to do, responsibilities to shoulder, promises to keep?*

*Do these make you feel fulfilled and truly content with your life?*

*If not, what needs to change? What is your inner voice telling you? (If you can hear it amidst all the turmoil that's going on in your head!)*

*Spend some time alone and think about what your vision is for your life. What are your goals? Yours, not anyone else's! Be ruthless in dealing with some of the things that take up your time, where you don't want them to. You may have to sacrifice a little income to gain this time, but the personal rewards can be great.*

*Write down everything you most want for yourself from your life. Some examples could be personal growth, financial freedom, adventure, a close and loving relationship with your partner, or good health and well-being. Spend some time doing this – it's important. Perhaps do it over a couple of weeks or so.*

*Now choose eight of the most significant items that you have written down and put them in order of what's most important to you. Then, using a scale of zero to ten, put a number next to each item that represents the priority you have given this item in the past three months. A score of zero means that you have not given any attention at all to the priority, and ten means giving it full attention.*

*Do you have any areas in your life where you are not spending your time doing what you feel is most important to you?*

*Are you spending time accomplishing other people's priorities, but not your own?*

*Carry your list of priorities with you wherever you go, and use it as a guideline for every demand made on your time. Stick it on your mirror so that you see it first thing in the morning and last thing at night.*

*Don't let anything come between you and what truly matters most to you!*

---

www.TheSharmaFoundation.org

www.dentabyte.co.uk

www.medibyte.com

www.SmileImpressions.com

Peter Thomson, Business and Personal Growth
Strategist

# So WHO Do YOU Trust If Not…?

Late afternoon on a dark and cold December day, 31st to be exact, the small boy, just 2 years and 3 months old, watched as his older sister warmed her cold-from-play hands in front of the rickety old, one-bar, electric heater.

**It was a time…** of self-reliance with the nanny-state not yet conceived, and one-bar electric heaters that didn't have guards. Fires did - but not the old one-bar, glowing red, 'oh so pretty' red bar hand-warmers.

The boy was fascinated to see his sister's face changing as her glowing cheeks turned redder and a slow smile of warmth spread across her face. Leaning forward, he copied what he'd seen. Don't all two-year olds? This is how they learn isn't it?

**He reached out…** for the pretty bar, and before anyone could stop him grabbed it with both hands.

**I don't remember the pain.** Presumably some inner part of my mind is protecting me from the memory. My mother told me I was in hospital for three months whilst skilled surgeons repaired my hands and readied me for the life ahead. By the age of seven, my hands had grown – but the skin grafts had not! My hands resembled a monkey's curved ones. The fingers wouldn't bend back with any ease. So off to the hospital again I went - this time only for a month and three days. More skin grafts, more stitches, more plaster casts. Oh, what fun trying to turn the pages of a book with plaster casts from finger tips to elbow!

As the scars healed - smaller casts, then large bandages, small bandages, then no bandages.

"*Come with me, Peter*", the nurse commanded. I did. Out of sight of anyone, in an empty ward, was a hand basin. "*Play with these Lux Flakes in this bowl of warm water; it will soften your hands. Stay here; do not move until I come back for you.*"

I stayed. And stayed. And stayed some more. The nurse forgot. I was there for 7 hours, 7 years old, 7 hours of memory.

I don't trust authority figures, never have; or at least not since that day. I ask questions to make them explain 'everything'. Nurses, doctors, airline pilots, police officers – the list is long. So glad she left me there – it's saved me so much heartache ever since.

So... WHO do YOU trust?

---

*Exercise:*

*Trust is a fundamental quality in all our relationships, both in our business and our personal lives.*

*Think of the people in your life that, no matter what time you call, if you need them, they will drop everything and support you – even at 3 in the morning!*

*They are the people who won't just tell you what you want to hear – they'll support you in making the right decisions for you.*

*What is it about these people that you trust?*

*Are their values aligned to your own?*

---

www.PeterThomson.com

*"We do not believe in ourselves until someone reveals that deep inside us something is valuable, worth listening to, worthy of our trust, sacred to our touch. Once we believe in ourselves we can risk curiosity, wonder, spontaneous delight or any experience that reveals the human spirit."*
E. E. Cummings

Kelly Morrisey, Author, Speaker, Divorce Recovery Coach

# A Better Life After Divorce

We all make mistakes - I make plenty of them. What really matters is how you learn from those mistakes.

You have a choice whether you will simply go through your divorce or grow through your past experiences. Divorce recovery and personal growth is all about learning how to turn self-defeating experiences into growth producing 'life-learning lessons.' Say to yourself, *"I want to grow and learn from my past experiences."*

One of the best things that you can do for yourself as you're recovering, growing, and moving forward in your new life is to reflect on what worked and what did not work in your marriage and in your other relationships. Taking an inventory is an honest effort at fact-finding and fact-facing. The object of taking a personal inventory is to disclose deep hidden thoughts or beliefs that are damaging your growth and remove them as swiftly as you can.

Resentment is usually the number one culprit. Take a separate sheet of paper, and answer these questions as best you can. You might decide to come back to them later as more is revealed.

What resentments are you holding onto?

Why are you angry?

Why are you holding on to them?

Holding on to resentments only hurts you; it doesn't hurt the offender. In fact, it eats away at your core. Holding on to deep resentments can adversely affect your happiness and satisfying relationships in your future. On the other hand, working through them and letting them go can help you become happier, stronger, and healthier.

Stop right here and take a moment to reflect on what has worked for you in the past and what hasn't worked for you.  For example:

| WHAT WORKED | WHAT DIDN'T WORK |
| --- | --- |
| Telling him that I was appreciative of what he did for me | Keeping my hurts and disappointments inside so they turned into resentment |
| Exercising at least 30 minutes to de-stress | Eating a pint of ice cream because I was trying to escape confrontation |
| Working through our issues together | Obsessing over past painful experiences |

Now it's your turn to write down what worked for you and what didn't work.

www.ABetterLifeAfterDivorce.com

www.ANewYouAfterDivorce.com (A community for those who are going, or have gone, through divorce)

*"Expect the best; convert problems into opportunities; be dissatisfied with the status quo; focus on where you want to go, instead of where you're coming from; and most importantly, decide to be happy, knowing it's an attitude, a habit gained from daily practice and not a result or payoff."*
Denis Waitley

# Success Principle #7:
# Plan And Take Action

- Work out a plan of action. This will give you:

  1. Direction and clarity

  2. A clearly defined measure of success

  3. A way to manage your time and resources

  4. Easier decision-making ability

- Break down the plan into baby steps.

- See the plan as an ongoing process that focuses on the results, and not on the individual elements, as measures of success. Take a step or two each day, reminding yourself that each step is bringing you closer to your goal.

- Perform each act to the best of your ability, filled with faith, determination and purpose to reach your goal.

- Most importantly, be consistent.

- However, be flexible enough to cope with changes. These could come in the form of competitor activity, or simply the fact that the plan is not working. Be honest though about the reasons why you are changing your plan. Don't change it just because something is proving to be a bit hard to do. Think outside the box – get someone else who is more of an expert in this area to do those tasks for you, while you concentrate on what you are good at.

- A well-constructed and thought out plan will help you to decide what to do within a context, i.e. what your vision is and what success will look like. If you keep that question at the forefront of all planning activity, it should guide you well.

- As Jane Lewis says in her Life Lesson: ***Make Your Goals SMART Ones***, … *"goals are generally useless if you don't take action to achieve them"*. A lesson that every co-author agrees with.

***"If you fail to plan, you plan to fail"***
Anon

Susanne Jorgensen, Psychologist, Coach, Author

# Don't Blame The Lettuce!

*"When you plant lettuce, if it does not grow well, you don't blame the lettuce. You look for reasons it is not doing well. It may need fertilizer, or more water, or less sun. You never blame the lettuce. Yet if we have problems with our friends or family, we blame the other person. But if we know how to take care of them, they will grow well, like the lettuce. Blaming has no positive effect at all, nor does trying to persuade using reason and argument. That is my experience. No blame, no reasoning, no argument, just understanding. If you understand, and you show that you understand, you can love, and the situation will change."*
Thich Nhat Hanh

I was working with a client who began sharing some issues he was struggling with in his relationship with his wife. They hadn't had a sexual relationship in a very long time. He told me that for the first three years after their child was born, they never once went out together as a couple, and now his wife wasn't interested in going away for a weekend break just with him. He felt like he was only good for bringing in the money and providing.

I spoke with another client who complained that her husband's job was all-consuming. He didn't have time for their children and they no longer did things as a couple. Even when he was home he was sitting at his laptop working. He would go away on weekends with his buddies or on ski and golf trips. He never bought my client so much as a birthday card or mother's day card – in fact he was often away on one of his own social trips.

*"Remember that our love for each other, like a beautiful tree, has to be watered, nurtured, loved and cared for in order for it to grow into a huge, full-blown lasting love."*
Susan Jeffers

I guess what amazes me is how little time and effort people put into their relationships – and then they wonder why they 'grow apart'. Busy couples spend their weekends not spending time together . . . sports matches, going out with friends, overworking, etc. So many couples squander their love by making other things more important. Over time, couples forget the nice things they did for each other. They stop celebrations of love they did when they first met – the gifts, surprises, the time and attention to each other.

Let's get real here. If you want love to grow and flourish, your relationship needs to be your top priority. Love isn't just an emotion, it's about action. 'Action or 'motion' is actually embedded in the word 'E*motion*'.

*"Relationships are either growing or dying. There is no middle ground. This is one of the governing principles of the universe. Everything is constantly changing."*
Matthew Kelly

Love expands when it's nurtured and contracts when it's neglected.

For most people, there is a huge gap between what they say is important and how they actually spend their lives. Life is priority driven. If you want to have an extraordinary relationship then you have to decide – you have to choose to make your relationship a priority. It's not enough to declare that your relationship is a priority – you have to actually make it a priority. Remember the saying: "*actions speak louder than words*"?

We all have three major resources – time, energy and money. How you spend your time, energy and money – not what you say - shows what your priorities are.

Every day we make choices and in making those choices, we are assigning a priority ranking to the different activities and relationships in our lives. Every day – consciously, or unconsciously, we are choosing.

The happiest people give focus and priority to their relationships. People who work harder and who work longer, perform better. It's true for athletes and for people in their businesses and careers. It's the same for relationships.

Great relationships are usually the ones where people work harder, work longer and as a result, have better relationships. Whether you have a great relationship or not has to do with you. It's your choice what you invest in. It's your choice how you use your time, energy and money. It's your choice whether you give your relationship the conditions for it to grow in. What you invest in is your choice.

At the end of the day, if you want your relationship to flourish and grow:

- You have to first decide which relationships matter the most

- You have to be willing to opt out of some relationships in order to give your most important ones time and attention

- You have to make loving actions a habit. There is no such thing as a 'little' gift – behind the gifts come the big message: I thought about you and I give you my love.

Remember this – if you aren't part of the solution, then you are part of the problem. Every moment is another chance to choose to turn things around.

No matter what state your relationship is in, it's never too late to turn things around.

---

*Exercise:*

*If you are serious about giving your relationship priority, you need to know what a great relationship looks like for you and also for your partner. Take some time to think about how you would define a great relationship – be as specific as you can. If you have a partner, ask them to do the same.*

- *How would you know you were enjoying being in a great relationship?*

- *How would you know you weren't enjoying being in a great relationship?*

- *For one or two weeks, track how you spend your time, energy and money. What does that say about what your priorities really are (not what you say they are)?*

- *If you do believe you are making your relationship a top priority, does your partner know and experience that?*

- *What are you doing to keep love alive?*

*(To get started with some ideas, see: www.LovingYou.com and '1001 Ways To Be Romantic' by Gregory P. J. Godek)*

---

Eve Grace-Kelly, Success Coach, Author

# Miscellaneous Life Lessons – Part III

Choosing which life lessons to include in the miscellaneous life lessons section has been hard. And, probably, some of our choices have been made because we've also learned them along the way. The first one here: "..... *it's taking me a long time to become the person I want to be.*" resonates with me. As a child, I was very shy – I was tall for my age, skinny, wore clothes that were made for me (not a cool thing!) and longed for the confidence and self-assurance I saw in others. Maybe I was a late developer, but it did happen.... eventually. I can confidently say, I am the person I want to be.

Which ones can you relate to or learn from? Tick those that apply and work on integrating the lessons into your own life.

| I've learned that............... | ✓ |
|---|---|
| .... it's taking me a long time to become the person I want to be. | |
| .... our heroes in life are people who do what has to be done when it needs to be done, regardless of the consequences. | |
| .... sometimes the people you expect to kick you when you're down, will be the ones to help you get back up. | |
| .... our background and circumstances may have influenced who we are, but we are responsible for who we become. | |
| .... two people can look at the same thing and see something totally different. | |
| .... no matter how much I care, some people just don't care back. | |
| .... you can do something in an instant that will give you heartache for life. | |
| .... learning to forgive takes practice. | |
| .... no matter how good a friend is, they're going to hurt you every once in a while and you must forgive them for that. | |
| .... maturity has more to do with what types of experiences you've had and what you've learned from them, and less to do with how many years you have lived. | |

Amanda van der Gulik, Entrepreneur,
Coach for Kids

# It's Your Choice!

Whatever happens in your life may not be your choice, but how you choose to react, is!

It's time to stop blaming others, or blaming our circumstances for how we are living. If you want to achieve your goals, if you want to live differently, if you want to be a different person....

That's your choice!

No-one can make that choice for you.

So where can you start to be in charge of your choices? How can you be in charge of how you react to your life?

Start with your mind. With your thoughts.

Whoever told you that you had to think a certain way? No-one else can hear your thoughts; they're yours. You have a choice as to the kind of thoughts you choose to entertain.

The way you think has a HUGE impact! And you're in full control.

It may not seem that way sometimes, but it really is up to you. Whenever you have a bad thought, you have the power to choose to say, "OUT!"

Whenever you have a good thought, you have the choice to say, "STAY!"

Stop letting others choose for you, but remember, if you don't take control of your own life, then you are letting others choose your outcomes for you.

It's enough! It's Your Choice!

*Exercise:*

*Think about how often your emotional reactions are automatic or on purpose. What percentage of the time would you attribute to each type of reaction?*

*Automatic [    %]        On purpose [    %]*

*Does your answer surprise you?*

*We all react to specific feelings that arise when something happens. And this is down to how we perceive the situation. Changing our perception will change our reaction, which, in turn will change the outcome of your feelings and actions – i.e. your experience in life.*

*Notice how you react to a given feeling. Think of a situation in the past where you reacted in a way you didn't want to. Write down what the feeling was and what contributed to it. What reaction would you have preferred?*

*The way we react is often linked to our values. When deciding how you would rather react, think about what reaction would serve the values you want to live by. How can you reduce the negative effects and increase the more desirable ones?*

*If your present reaction is generally one of anger or frustration, are these feelings what you want in your life? If not, what other type of reaction would be more aligned to your values or how you want to live your life?*

*By noticing your feelings, you can take control and eliminate the experience and results of your anger or frustration (or whatever other feelings you don't want) in a given situation. Take command of your thinking and choose how you want to direct it. Determine what you DO want in your life.*

www.GetUnstuckForKids.com

*"Our reactions to our feelings are our passport to rebirth."*
Ayya Khema, *Being Nobody, Going Nowhere*

Debbie Allen, The Millionaire Entrepreneur
Business Builder

# Develop A Positive Belief System About Promoting YOU

*"If you don't toot your own horn, you can't enjoy the music."*
Debbie Allen

Self-promotion, when done effectively, works for ANY business or career. Once you begin to implement the proven marketing strategies behind it … it's EASY to be successful in anything you set your mind to. In fact, when you promote yourself over and over again, you will begin to enjoy it more, and it will reward you many times over in return.

I shockingly discovered that an average of 87% of the thousands of business people I've surveyed, did NOT feel comfortable promoting themselves and avoided it MOST of the time. In business, we understand that if we don't promote and market we can't be successful. Right? No matter how great your service is or what amazing value you offer, if prospects don't know about you, you're not going to win the opportunity to do business with them. Therefore, if you don't promote yourself … it goes against the grain of all sales and marketing success! Right?

But why do so many people feel uncomfortable with self-promotion? Because … much of what they believe to be true about self-promotion comes from past programming that dates back to their childhood. When you grew up you may have heard comments like: *"It's not polite to talk about yourself. It will come across as pushy or rude."*

Too many of us have 10, 20, 30 or more years of negative and/or limiting beliefs rattling around in our heads about the concept of self-promotion. These limiting and negative beliefs have been programmed into our subconscious minds for years. What were your parents, teachers or guardians like when you were growing up? Did they believe in promoting themselves? Did they promote your self-esteem to believe that you could do anything you set your mind to? Were they risk-takers, or were they conservative? We usually hate to admit it, but we are all creatures of habit, especially when habits have been programmed into our brains since childhood. Some people are so conditioned against self-promotion they are closed minded about it; no matter how much it might benefit them. Now, I don't expect you to change your beliefs overnight, but you can start by opening your mind to believing differently about self-promotion from this day forward.

Why believe differently? Because you can't be truly successful if you aren't willing to let people know that you, your product and/or services exist. If you aren't willing to promote your talents, expertise and products, others will quickly pass you by. The world is not going to beat a path to your door unless you pave the way. Resenting self-promotion is one of the greatest obstacles to success.

www.SalesandMarketingSuccess.com

*"The most notable winners usually encountered heartbreaking obstacles before they triumphed. They won because they refused to become discouraged."*
B.C. Forbes

Janet Beckers, Internet Marketing Expert, Speaker, Author, Mentor

# Always Choose The Challenging Path

Just over three years ago, I made a decision. A decision that would change my life forever.

I was sitting in the audience of an Internet marketing conference. I had been learning about different ways to build an Internet-based business for years and, even though I had been applying what I was learning, I had not had the success I wanted. As I watched speaker after speaker share their story, a thought suddenly struck me. Every single one of these people on stage at some point had made the choice to really push themselves out of their comfort zones. They had chosen to tread the scary path.

Sitting in the back of the room, I made my decision. I promised myself that, whenever I was faced with a choice of two ways to do something: one way that I felt confident to do and another that really pushed me out of my comfort zone but, potentially, would give a better result, I would always, always choose the challenging path. I have stayed true to my promise to myself and it is this one decision that I credit with my snowballing path to success. Of course, not every choice is successful, but every time I push myself out of my comfort zone, my confidence increases. This makes the next challenge seem less daunting. Three years later, I find myself taking on challenges I never would have thought I was capable of. I am very excited about what my future holds.

---

*Exercise:*

*Make a promise to yourself now. Right now.*

*Write it down if you need to and put the paper somewhere you will see it often. Read it aloud first thing in the morning and last thing at night.*

*"I will always choose the option that really pushes me out of my comfort zone."*

---

# Success Principle #8:
# Commit To Action – Be Passionate!

- Passion and Commitment ignite action.

- Commitment requires you to consistently practice your beliefs.

- Success requires both commitment and a determination to honor that commitment.

- Dig deep into your inner power and take whatever steps you need to take to help you achieve your goals.

- Too often, we find it easy to keep our commitments to others while neglecting to keep our commitments to ourselves. Be selfish once in a while.

- Don't procrastinate - procrastinators are experts in creating excuses. As Gurbaksh Chahal, in his Life Lesson #22 *Living The Dream*, says, "*Procrastination is just another word for wanting to fail. If you're not hungry enough, if you're too lazy to move forward, you're never going to get anywhere*".

- Day-to-day, commitment is demonstrated by a combination of two actions:

   1. **Supporting**. Genuine support develops a commitment in the minds and hearts of others. Focus on what is important and lead by example. Concentrate on what adds value. Stand up to those who undermine your commitment.

   2. **Improving**, which takes our commitment to an even higher level. Look for better ways to do things and learn from the process. Challenge current expectations and take the risk to make changes. Change should be based more on optimism about the future rather than dissatisfaction with the past.

- Richard Branson, Bill Gates, Donald Trump and Warren Buffett, to name a few, all have the money they will ever need, but they still carrying on working - why? Because they are passionate about what they do. They do not consider what they do as 'work'. This kind of passion breeds success.

*When the car-maker, Professor Porsche was asked what his favorite model was in the long line of Porsche automobiles, he replied: "I haven't built it yet!"*

*Commitment is "persistence with a purpose".*

*"The man who succeeds above his fellows is the one who, early in life, clearly discerns his object and towards that object habitually directs his powers; even genius is nothing but fine observation strengthened by fixity of purpose. Every man who observes vigilantly and resolves steadfastly, grows unconsciously into genius."*
Bulwer

Marie O'Riordan, Communications Excellence
Specialist

# It's OK To Be Different

I'm grateful for having the courage to take the road less travelled in
my life.

The unpredictability and spontaneity of my decisions have seen me
guided to experiences that very few humans ever get to enjoy.

Please read with me...

> *'I know that from today everything is going to be O.K.*
> *even when I choose to do what others*
> *would never be brave enough to decide to do.'*

> *"Enter through the narrow gate. For wide is the gate and broad*
> *is the road that leads to destruction, and many enter through it.*
> *But small is the gate and narrow is the road that leads to life,*
> *and only a few find it."*
> Matthew 7:13-14

---

*Exercise:*

*In life, there are two paths available to each of us – the Broad road
and the Narrow road. Which path we choose to go down is determined
by our own actions, our decisions, and our priorities. It is decided by
our character – the ability to make the right choice, even if it is not the
easy choice.*

*The Broad road is often known as 'the path of least resistance.' Here,
we often compromise our beliefs, or we may not even realize what
is important to us. We don't have to make difficult decisions, and
sometimes give up our decision-making to others. Travelling down this
road often leaves us unfulfilled.*

*Taking the Narrow road can be the more difficult choice. It can often
mean that you need to be selfless and have an element of personal*

*awareness. It involves giving of yourself for the good of others. Although taking the Narrow road can be a challenge, it is full of rewards along the way that provide great happiness and fulfillment.*

*Think about the following scenarios:*

- If you were to see a colleague engaging in unethical behavior at work, do you ignore the behavior (i.e. take the Broad road), or do you feel compelled to speak to the colleague or to their manager (i.e. taking the Narrow road)?

- When you are tired and your son asks you to play ball with him, what is your reaction? Do you choose the Broad road and give him something else to do, or do you take the Narrow road and go out and play ball with him in the garden, and savor the opportunity to play and build your relationship with him?

*These types of decisions crop up every now and then and it's useful to know how you recognize the difference between the Broad road and the Narrow road. How do you know which one you are on, or which one to take? Do the actions you are currently taking provide any benefit to others? This is particularly important when it comes to decisions regarding family. The person who is serious about personal development will make the choice that benefits the family.*

*Another simple way to realize the difference is to ask yourself whether you are being asked to do something difficult. If you can honestly say you have a difficult task or a tough decision to make, you are being asked to choose which path to take.*

*The most important aspect of personal development with regard to the Narrow road is wanting to make the difficult decision. When this happens, you realize the value in traveling the narrow road and are open to the wondrous experiences traveling this little inhabited path might provide. You realize that life cycles through prosperity and challenge, and you are open to fully experiencing both.*

---

www.MarieORiordanInternational.com

Eve Grace-Kelly, Success Coach, Author

# The 80/20 Rule – Use Your Time Wisely

I'm a self-confessed perfectionist, and sometimes need to check myself to ensure that I'm giving the right amount of attention to tasks depending on their priority.

Studies have shown that 20% of your activities are likely to produce 80% of the *meaningful* outcomes in your life.

---

*Exercise:*

*Write down the 20% of your activities that are likely to bring you the most important results in your life.*

*What are the three things in your list that will make the biggest impact, give you the best results and help you to move to where you want to be in your life, career or business?*

*The more time you spend on these three activities, the more productively your time will be spent and the quicker you will achieve your results.*

*Don't waste time on activities that will not move you towards your end goal.*

*Beware of 'displacement activities', i.e. those things that you do to avoid tackling the harder stuff....*

*If you play to your strengths, i.e. the things that you do best, things will be easier and your time will be even more productively spent.*

---

www.QCCGroup.com

Toby Garbett, Olympian

# Control The Controllables

When in a professional or amateur-based sport, or even if you are in a business situation, it is always important to be aware of the competition and use them as a springboard for you to improve and do better. However, time and time again, you see people panicking and looking out of the corner of their eye or over their shoulder at what other people are doing. In doing this, they lose focus on where they are headed and what they can control.

You can't control other people's actions but knuckle down and do the best that you can and the outcome is the outcome.

---

*Exercise:*

*Even if you don't have 100% control over some things that happen in your work or personal life, there are some strategies that you can use:*

*Ask yourself:*

- *Who do I control (at work or elsewhere)?*

- *Who do I not control?*

- *What do I control?*

- *What do I not control?*

*Typically, you'll find that your answers regarding who or what you can't control involve others, or things, outside yourself. And that the only person or things that you can have control over (either partially or totally) involve yourself. You can't control things like the world's supply of energy, inflation, recession, the weather, or what other people say and do. You might be able to reduce your energy consumption, etc.*

*but even though you're affected by those things, and you want to do something about them, you're not really responsible for them. There's a big difference.*

*So what are the things that deserve your focus and attention? The things you CAN control.*

*This really comes down to **your** self-improvement, **your** attitude, **your** values, **your** goals, **your** opportunity awareness, **your** focus, **your** disciplined use of time, **your** commitment, **your** enthusiasm, **your** knowledge, **your** persistence, **your** preparation, etc.*

*These really are **your** responsibilities and are the things that **you** CAN control.*

---

www.TobyGarbett.com

*"First, recognize that you are not a sheep who will be satisfied with only a few nibbles of dry grass or with following the herd as they wander aimlessly, bleating and whining, all of their days. Separate yourself now from the multitude of humanity so that you will be able to control your own destiny. Remember that what others think and say and do need never influence what you think and say and do."*
Og Mandino

Stephanie Hale, Publishing Expert and
Writing Coach

# The Small Things Are
# The Big Things

It was a hot muggy day, the trains were running late, and I had
childcare issues before I left.

I was attending a business workshop in London and I arrived feeling
more than a little frazzled.

Not only this, but the majority of attendees at this workshop failed to
turn up. So of the 12 expected, there were only two of us – myself and
another attendee.

The promoter was clearly not expecting this. He had prepared a day
of exercises and strategies aimed at 12 people... but he battled on
valiantly.

I attend many such events as part of my business education. Some
events are brilliant, filled with 'Aha' moments. Others are 'OK', but
nothing to shout about. This workshop was of the latter variety – and
to be honest, I had all but forgotten it.  Except that nearly 12 months
on, I received an email from that other single attendee. He was writing
to thank me for the parting hug I gave him, and for helping to make a
difference after a nightmare period in his life.

*"Your words and the hugging gave me power to come through. You
don't have to understand this, but it helped me,"* he wrote.

Unknown to me, this business owner was going through a huge
trauma in his life. I have to say he hid it well – I hadn't a clue at
the time. But it struck me when I received his touching note how
important warmth is... how smiles and hugs can make such a huge
difference.

I'm a tactile person. I enjoy my life and the people who surround me.
So it feels natural for me to embrace the people I meet. Sometimes
just a smile, eye contact and a touch on the arm is enough to lift
someone's spirits.

It's the small things that count every single day... even at dull business workshops on sweltering days when you'd much rather be somewhere else.

---

*Exercise:*

*Spend a day smiling at strangers in the street and hugging the people around you.*

*Make a mental note of how good this makes you feel!*

---

www.MillionaireWomenMillionaireYou.com/free

www.MillionaireWomenResources.com

*"We must not, in trying to think about how we can make a big difference, ignore the small daily differences we can make which, over time, add up to big differences that we often cannot foresee."*
Marian Wright Edelman

Paul Avins, The Turbo Business Coach, Author,
International Speaker, Entrepreneur

# If You Want To Earn More You Must Learn More …

*"Work harder on yourself than you do on your Job or Business…"*
Jim Rohn

Having struggled in the early stages of my life with dyslexia and the learning challenges it gave me - I could not read at the age of eight - I had lost all belief in the traditional education system.

Then at the age of 19, I met a mentor who had huge success in his personal and business life and shared with me a powerful life lesson – *"Invest 10% of what you earn every year back into educating your biggest asset, YOU."*

I was smart enough to take this advice on board and even during very tough personal financial situations, I keep investing in books, CDs and training courses…. even when others close to me thought I was crazy and could not afford it. My mindset was that I couldn't afford NOT to invest in me - as clearly I didn't know the right information to get the results I wanted.

You have already proved you are in the top 10% of your field or industry by investing in this book and I applaud you for your commitment to grow.

Use these simple but powerful questions below to get clarity on what you need to learn next to go the next level. After all, you have to **BE**come better before you can **DO** what's needed to **HAVE** the results you want.

*Exercise:*

- *What areas of your Life or Business are underperforming right now?*

- *What books could you read to learn more about this area?*

- *What course could you take or seminar could you attend?*

- *Is there a Coach or Mentor who could help you grow your skills faster?*

www.TheBusinessWealthClub.com

www.Paul-Avins.com

*"We are born into a vast room whose walls consist of a thousand doors of possibility. Each door is flung open to the world outside, and the room is filled with light and noise. We close some of the doors deliberately, sometimes with fear, sometimes with calm certainty. Others seem to close by themselves, s ome so quietly that we do not even notice."*

Terry Teachout

Kathleen Ronald, Networker, Speaker, Trainer, Consultant

# Make Forgiveness Your Friend!

*"Forgiveness is the medicine to heal your hurts before they kill you."*
Kathleen Ronald

As a business consultant and trainer, I've worked with many clients on the topic of Forgiveness and I've studied it in numerous philosophies as I too have found situations where it was hard to forgive. Forgiveness can be a very complex issue. I write in my poem entitled 'Are You Ready?'

**"Clear your heart as it still aches in ways
that you have yet to address!"**

It's the ego, working to protect us. It hangs on and keeps us fired up, causing us to eat angry pie (always a bestseller), resentment pie, bitter pie, hate pie (close cousin to angry pie) and all the other negative emotions we experience when we cannot arrive at forgiveness. Without providing any benefit, too much pie causes us to die way before our time.

In *Fire In The Soul: A New Psychology of Spiritual Optimism*, Joan Borysenko, PhD explains:

*"Forgiveness is not the misguided act of condoning irresponsible, hurtful behavior. Nor is it a superficial turning of the other cheek that leaves us feeling victimized and martyred. Rather, it is the finishing of old business that allows us to experience the present, free of contamination from the past."*

The one exercise that supported me to stop eating emotional pies was given to me by Reverend Michael Beekwith of Agape in Culver City, California. He said, *"The definition of forgiveness is this...*

*Thank you for giving me..."*

WOW! This reframing freed me to heal those parts of my heart that held onto hatred, anger, blame and their other cousins. It feels like these thoughts and emotions would help us, but they only make us sick and tired. I realized that, in not forgiving, I was choosing to give away my power, joy, freedom, love - and so much more.

When you take the lessons from the situations or persons, you forgive them, bless them and let them prosper elsewhere.

Get the GOLD (the lessons) from the act of for-giving... it WILL change your life!

---

*Exercise:*

*In what ways does your heart ache?*

*Whom and what do you need to forgive?*

*Make a list of each person that you 'get' to forgive. Do one person at a time and write..."John, thank YOU FOR GIVING ME...." and let the lessons flow.*

*Be sure to include yourself!*

---

www.Speaktacular.com

*FORGIVE and FEEL the freedom!*

*"I can forgive, but I cannot forget, is only another way of saying, I will not forgive. Forgiveness ought to be like a cancelled note - torn in two, and burned up, so that it never can be shown against one."*
Henry Ward Beecher

# Success Principle #9:
## Stay Focused

- The key here is to direct your attention (or focus) on coordinating all the faculties of your mind and direct their combined power to a specific end.

- Toby Garbett states, in his Life Lesson: **Mental Toughness**, *"Focus on your desired results. Do what's necessary now and stay in the present. By not worrying about what happened yesterday or what is going to happen tomorrow, two-thirds of your worries simply disappear!"*

- Keep your mind ON the things you want and OFF the things you don't want.

- It is much easier to focus your attention on something you believe will happen than on something you believe is unlikely.

- The positive mental attitude in Success Principle #1 will support you in this. Positive and negative emotions cannot occupy your mind at the same time. One or other must dominate.

- Detach from negative thoughts - your thoughts can't hold any power over you if you don't judge them. If you notice yourself having a negative thought, detach from it, witness it, and don't follow it. Rejection isn't real; it is our imaginary perception of an event we have experienced. The next time you feel rejected, remind yourself you have the power to change that perception, and thus change the feeling as well.

*"It's not what's happening to you now or what has happened in your past that determines who you become. Rather, it's your decisions about what to focus on, what things mean to you, and what you're going to do about them that will determine your ultimate destiny."*
Anthony Robbins

Emma Tiebens, Relational Marketer

# Have A Positive
# Influence On People

*"Do you leave people better than you found them?"*
John Mason

I remember as a young girl growing up in Manila, Philippines, that I was fascinated by older people. I loved watching them and seeing how they interacted, what they said to each other and whether they were authentic and genuine, or whether they were just doing it for small talk.

My Mom is very traditional and old fashioned and is something of a 'people pleaser'. It's so important to her for people only to say nice things about us and our family. So the whole family, including myself and my three siblings, made sure that we always acted accordingly, never giving anyone a chance to say anything bad about her parenting skills. Little did I know that such discipline would have a profound impact in my life! I grew up to be a 'people pleaser', but certainly not in the way of sacrificing my decisions and opinions for the sake of pleasing everyone. The gem that I got out of that was simple: *"Do I leave people better than I found them?"* Would my interaction with them - even for a brief moment - make a difference in their lives even for but a split second?

How would the world be if we all become genuinely interested in the other person without any expectation, other than to show that they matter and they exist? Perhaps there will be less egotistical *"I'm better than you..."* sort of thing. It's a combination of being present... being genuinely interested in them and really having the desire to get to know them at a deeper level.

Now, as the Founder of The Relational Marketer, it is my mission to *'Encourage, Empower and Engage Entrepreneurs'.* I guess the young people-pleasing girl has found a way to show genuine interest in people by teaching other entrepreneurs how they too can do the same. The question I normally ask is, *"Whose Life Is Now Better Because Of Yours?"*

*Exercise:*

1) *Be generous with your compliments, but don't use flattery.*

2) *Ask people questions about their family - that's always a great conversation starter!*

3) *The person asking the question controls the conversation. Avoid saying, "Oh yes, I had the same experience and here's what happened..." Be a genuine listener, not just someone who waits for something in common to engage in the conversation - it's easier to relate to someone just like you, but there are more benefits in engaging with someone who's not like you.*

4) *Use their names often in the conversation... before you know it, you would have remembered their name effortlessly!*

www.TheRelationalMarketer.com

*"You need only choose... then keep choosing as many times as necessary. That is all you need do. And it is certainly something you can do. Then as you continue to choose, everything is yours."*
Vernon Howard

Dr Jane Lewis, Career Coach

# The World Is Your Barometer

*"He who wrestles with us strengthens our nerves and sharpens our skill. Our antagonist is our helper."*
Edmund Burke (1729 - 1797)

The way we experience the world around us offers us a wonderful barometer for what's going on inside at an unconscious level. If you've ever wondered why you're not getting the results you want in life, or if you've ever felt that other people seem to be luckier than you, or doing better than you, or if you get judgmental about other people's behaviors, then you can treat that as useful information that tells you what you need to work on.

This concept is often known as *'perception is projection'*, and you will often hear coaches and others tie it in to the Jungian concept of the shadow self. The basic idea is that when you experience something outside yourself – whether you see it, hear it, or come across it in some other way – if it fires off an emotional charge in you, then you yourself are, at some level, and in some way, behaving like that.

For example, if you find that you get annoyed or upset by someone behaving in a bigoted way, it indicates that, at some level, somewhere in your life, you act like a bigot. If you asked yourself, *"what does bigoted mean to me?"*, you might come up with an answer like *'intolerance'*. The question then is, where in your life are you being intolerant, and with whom? And if you find yourself saying things like, *"I would never be bigoted"* or *"Bigotry is just plain wrong,"* then you have work to do.

If you find yourself envying people their results, then it's probably time to think about how you set goals and how committed you are to achieving them – but that's a story for another chapter.

---

*Exercise:*

Next time you find yourself getting upset by someone else's behaviour, ask yourself, what does that behaviour mean to me or represent for me? Where in my life do I do that, and to whom?

The answer may surprise you.

---

www.TheCareerSuccessDoctor.com

> *"Be the change you wish to see in the world.*
> Mahatma Ghandi"

> *"The past does not equal the future. Because you may have failed a moment ago, all day today, or for the last 6 months, or for the last sixteen years, or for the last fifty years of your life doesn't mean anything. All that matters is what are you going to do now?"*
> Anthony Robbins

Eve Grace-Kelly, Success Coach, Author

# Coping In A Man's World (Or Is It?!)

One of the challenges I've had to face over the whole of my working life has been that of the fact that many industries are male-dominated. It's less the case now than it was 3 decades ago I agree, but in many cases, it's still prevalent.

One of the interesting tests has been, not only working amongst men, but when called upon to manage them that the male-female dynamics come into play! Thankfully, a number of years spent in the field of Human Resources early on in my career gave me an interest in self-help or personal development that I've continued to this day. Our library of books in this niche is pretty extensive. (Nine bookcases at the last count, with more space being needed!)

Training in Neuro-Linguistic Programming has enhanced my interpersonal skills, teaching me about body language, communication skills, and so forth. My schooling as a Coach has also added to my repertoire of tools and techniques for improved team-work and good relationships.

As a member of the Association of Project Managers' Special Interest Group, Women In Project Management, I was invited to lecture them in London on Personal Energy Management. I surveyed my audience and found that they still shared many of the problems I'd faced over the years, with new challenges arising such as multi-cultural relationship issues. Working with over 40 member countries of a pan-European organization as a Programme Management consultant in Brussels had taught me a lot about that!

An interesting experience, though, was a conversation I had with a colleague many years ago. We had been recruited into similar roles within just a few months of each other. We got on quite well, but I always detected there was something not quite right with the relationship – I just couldn't put my finger on what was wrong. I was friendly and inclusive, so what was wrong? Well, we bumbled along for a while until my curiosity got the better of me. I went to lunch with my colleague and voiced my unease.

The nub of his angst was that I (a woman) was recruited onto a higher grade than he (a man) was and therefore was earning a higher salary..... Well, you could have knocked me over with a feather! It had never occurred to me that that was the problem. I had been working in male-dominated environments for a while and, whilst I knew I had to go the extra mile to be noticed (remember, I'm shy at this point!), I had never previously been in a position where I was actually the higher paid.

Good relationships in our personal and working lives are extremely important and I wanted to improve this one. We talked about why he felt the way he did, the impact his thoughts had on our relationship, and, given the fact that I wasn't going to ask my manager for a reduced salary, how we could resolve the situation. In this case, things improved having aired the problem and we became good friends.

I'm passionate about self-improvement and personal growth and firmly believe that there are tons of tools and techniques available with which to overcome many work-based challenges for women, whether in project management or any other arena where men and women work together. www.WomenInProjectManagement.com focuses exclusively on the needs of women Project or Programme Managers, Planners and other Project or Programme Office staff. Here, we examine what the struggles or obstacles are that you need to overcome in your working life and exactly how to do that.

For women in general, outside the project management sphere, check out this fantastic resource offering career advice, personal development tips, problem-sharing and other hot topics of interest to women:www.MillionaireWomenResources.com. Together with Stephanie Hale, one of our superb co-authors, we showcase a number of other highly successful international women from this book and elsewhere. They share their secrets for success and how to overcome obstacles that get in the way.

www.QCCGroup.com

Andy Harrington, Peak Performance Specialist

# A Message From Above

*"Remember that nothing ever truly dies.*
*All things are constantly in a state of transformation"*
Andy Harrington

The 21st November, 2001 started out pretty much the same as every other day; and then something happened that I would remember forever.

I received a phone call from my business partner, George, in some distress, asking me if I could drive his partner Nicola to the hospital as soon as possible, as her mum had just had a heart attack and he wasn't nearby.

Within a few minutes, Nicola and I were on the way to the Queen Mary Hospital in Sidcup, Kent, UK, but alas we were not there in time for Nicola to see her mum alive again as she had already passed away.

Later that evening, I returned home having spent all day with Nicola and George, just being a good friend and supporting them the best I could. I drew a warm bath to comfort myself after a difficult day. Within a few moments, I had this sudden urge to get out of the bath and write down a few thoughts. I can only describe the feeling as one of compulsion; it was as if I was running on autopilot.

Five minutes later, I had written the words of a poem that left me speechless. You see, the thing is, I don't write poetry, apart from a few awkward attempts in a Valentine's card.

The next morning, I was in a dilemma. Should I give the poem to Nicola or not? The words of the poem were so personal, I didn't know if it was the right thing to do. But the only way I could rationalize what happened was that, somehow, Nicola's mum had found a way of sending a message to her daughter through me.

I printed the poem out, framed it nicely, and met with Nicola to give her the poem and explain what had happened. As she read the words of the poem, she began to cry and, for a moment, I began to regret my decision, thinking that perhaps it was too early for her to read words such as these.

When she had finished reading, she hugged me and said it was just what she needed. Within days, I had supplied a copy to every member of the family.

*I am the wind,*
*I am the rain,*
*I am the sunlight through your windowpane,*
*I am the leaf turning brown in the fall,*
*I'm the faintest whisper on the breeze when you call.*

*I am the snowflake that kisses your cheek,*
*I'm the child in the park playing hide-and-go-seek,*
*I'm the scent of the flowers that fill the spring air,*
*I'm all around you,*
*I'm everywhere.*

*I'll always be with you from this moment on,*
*In your every dance,*
*Your every song.*

*You see when you move on,*
*We never truly die,*
*We become one with nature,*
*We unify.*

*Take care my precious one,*
*On my passing don't dwell,*
*Remember the love we shared together,*

*See you again someday,*
*All is well.*

This experience changed my beliefs about spirituality and was instrumental in guiding me to become a motivational speaker and transform the lives of people throughout the world through my work.

I have now set the words of the poem to stunning photography and moving music. If you would like to see it, you can do that here. www.MessagesOfSympathy.com

*Exercise:*

*Light a room by candlelight and sit cross-legged opposite someone close enough so you can touch each other. Go into peripheral vision by looking in between the eyes of the other person and stare for three minutes. During this time, get yourself into a loving state and send loving thoughts to the other person.*

*For many people when they carry out this exercise, they report they see the faces of many other people, including, many times, those who have passed.*

www.PowerToAchieve.co.uk/freedvd

*"Whenever you have an opportunity to laugh, laugh;
whenever you have an opportunity to dance, dance;
whenever you have an opportunity to sing, sing -
and one day you will find you have created your paradise."*
Osho, Indian Spiritual Teacher

Nick James, Business Coach, Speaker, Internet Marketer

# Look At Success And Failure In The Same Light

I've always believed that it's vitally important to look at success and failure in the same light – and to realize that it's okay to try, and fail, on the road to achieving your dreams, because experience is never wasted.

One of my favorite stories to take heart from relates to Thomas Edison. When asked about his long road to inventing the light bulb, he replied:

*"I have not failed 1,000 times.*
*I have successfully discovered 1,000 ways to NOT make a light bulb."*

This just about sums up everything you need to know about succeeding in business, and in life.

Each time you make an honest attempt and try your best, you're one step further to getting there – and every valuable mistake you make helps you along your way to succeeding.

---

*Exercise:*

*In the 1950s, the Jacuzzi brothers invented a whirlpool bath to treat people with arthritis. The product worked, but from a sales perspective, it flopped as very few people in the target market, sufferers from arthritis, could afford the expensive bath. It only became a success once they relaunched the same product for a different market – as a luxury item for the wealthy. As we all know, it became a huge success!*

*This is a great success story out of what looked like failure...............*

*A great way to learn from our 'failures' is to keep a journal and write about our experiences.*

*Keep track of everything that happens to you – it's a great way to reflect on and express how a failure has impacted your life.*

*When writing about your failures, there are two key questions to ask:*

*1. Why did this happen?*

*2. What good might come from it?*

*The second question, in particular, seeks out the potential success from failure.*

*There is no failure – only learning..........*

---

www.Nick-James.com

*"Why let others define success for you?*
*Here are two insights that can allow you to live successfully:*
*1) Compete only with your own best self*
*2) Steadily move toward your own worthwhile goals."*
Martha Reid

Emma Tiebens, Relational Marketer

# "Invest In YOU, Inc.... The Returns Are Enormous!"

Mike Dillard

Two years ago, I was searching for the 'Holy Grail' of online marketing and I came across a gentleman by the name of Mike Dillard. He was the Founder of Magnetic Sponsoring™ and in five short years, was able to create a multi-million dollar company selling information online!

What's *Magnetic Sponsoring™*? It is Mike Dillard's *'how to'* guide for people who want to become attractive as leaders and position themselves in places of influence and become 'Alpha Networkers'. I absolutely highly recommend anyone who has a business and is thinking of going online to start with this book, as this will set you apart from those who will be drowned in the noise because they will fail to position themselves with the proper posture.

Investing in YOU, Inc. What does that really mean? Well, it's knowing where to allocate limited financial and time resources! In my case, it was realizing early on whether to buy that Louis Vuitton® purse I've been eyeing at the LV® Store in South Coast Plaza, or invest in a Traffic Formula Course... it's investing $5,000 to be able to get one-on-one coaching from the Quantum Leap Coach, Tracy Repchuk, or taking my family on a Mexican Riviera Cruise? It's the choice between being up-to-date with the episodes of *Desperate Housewives* or spending more time listening to recorded webinars that teach skills and leads conversion?

I could have found all the excuses in the book as to why I couldn't afford the courses, the seminars, the coaches, but I learned early on that it is critical that I invest in ME, Inc! If I didn't, then I might as well have said "goodbye" to my dreams. Investing in YOU, Inc. will take you places you've never been before, unlock doors you wouldn't have otherwise seen and connect with people you wouldn't have met before!

---

*Exercise:*

1)  Go to Amazon.com - search for books in your chosen industry and your expertise.

2) Identify leaders whom you want to emulate or be mentored by.

3) Use social media to connect with industry leaders, join their Group or Fan Pages.

4) Search for what your Mentors are offering by way of Free Reports, etc.

5) Find out where their seminars are, purchase their course and start implementing what you've learned.

6) Train yourself to identify the key players you ultimately would like to become your peers.

7) Create relationships with them - reach out to them online, attend their live webinars, opt in to their email list and, attend a LIVE event they are hosting and meet them in person!

---

www.TheRelationalMarketer.com

*"The minute you settle for less than you deserve,
you get even less than you settled for."*
Maureen Dowd

Amanda van der Gulik, Entrepreneur,
Coach for Kids

# The Bitter May Surprise You!

Life has a way of sending us our lessons. We learn best by our mistakes and by life's disasters.

If our lives were always perfect and sweet, we would never learn, never grow. It's part of our requirements here on earth to live the best we can and to learn the most we can to better ourselves.

Sometimes, life can feel at an absolute bottom. We find ourselves financially stressed, or we lose a loved one.

It's hard to see in the moment, but if we just allow the healing process to carry us forward, a lesson can always be found.

With money, maybe we have been keeping it away by how we've been feeling inside – through a feeling of being unworthy of success? Or perhaps a belief of simply not being clever enough?

Well this is simply not true! These are restrictions (or limiting beliefs) we have put upon ourselves, maybe because we've heard others say them to us, but that doesn't mean they're true.

What is true is what we believe. Bitter moments can be horrible or they can be a blessing in disguise to reveal themselves in time.

Maybe a loved one passes on way too early in life. Yes, that is tragic. But it has happened. You cannot turn back the clock.

What you can do is take it as a life lesson to make sure that you live your own life to its fullest so that when your time comes to move on to the other side, you'll look back and smile; you lived!

Don't let the bitter moments of life stop you. There really is something good in everything.

www.AllowanceSecrets.com

# Success Principle #10: Budget Your Time, Energy And Money

- Manage your personal energy. (Take the **Personal Energy Management** test in Eve Grace-Kelly's Life Lesson.)

- Take a regular inventory of yourself to learn how and where you are spending your time, your energy and your money.  As Gill Fielding says in her Life Lesson: **The Financial Recipe**, *"Control the flow of money through your life…. Keep re-investing any profit or surplus you make…..Get control of debt…. Keep tweaking your personal financial recipe…. Grasp every opportunity you can… Invest in a spread of things… Make the money flow passively into your life."*

- Time is too precious to be wasted on arguments and discontent. Some mistakes can be corrected, but not the mistake of wasting time.  When time is gone, it's gone forever.

- The secret of getting things done is: DO IT NOW!

## The Ribbon Of Time

- Take a ribbon (or piece of string) of about one meter in length. It doesn't really matter how long, but this is just a guide.  This represents your lifespan, so decide how long you want to live (or think you will live!).  Of course, this cannot be exact – think of an aspirational age.

- Holding the ribbon ends in each hand, fold it at a point to indicate your current age (e.g. if you are now 50 years old and you hope to live to be 100, fold it in half).  Let your 'age part' hang loose. *This part of your life has gone and can never be regained.  However, you do have the memories and lessons that you have learned along the way to take forward with you into the rest of your life.*

- Choose how much time you are going to spend asleep during the rest of your life. Measure this along your Ribbon of Time and let this part hang loose.

- Decide how much time you are going to spend carrying out day-to-day activities such as showering, cooking, eating, shopping, etc. and measure this out on your Ribbon of Time – let this part hang loose.

- What's left is the amount of time you have left to invest or exchange for whatever you want to do, things you want to achieve, time you want to spend with people who are important to you, experiences you want to have.

- Invest it well – once spent, you can never regain it!

*"It's not enough to be busy, so are the ants.
The question is, what are we busy about?"*
Henry David Thoreau

Stephanie Hale, Publishing Expert and Writing Coach

# Making A Breakthrough

Just a short bike ride away from my home is the track where Roger Bannister broke the 4-minute mile.

Until the record was broken, everyone believed it was beyond human ability. His rival, John Landy, had tried – and failed – on six occasions. He told Bannister it just wasn't possible. This was the widespread belief.

Bannister changed all that in 1954, by finishing in 3 minutes 59.4 seconds.

Now here's the significant bit. Within six weeks of the barrier being broken, Landy did the run in 3 minutes 57.9 seconds. Many other runners followed suit, and today, many ordinary club athletes can beat Bannister's time.

Did athletes suddenly evolve with longer legs and stronger muscles? Unlikely. The barrier was psychological as much as physical.

Once someone established a strong enough belief that it could be done, the 'impossible' became 'possible'. This clearly shows how limiting beliefs can hold people back from achieving their full potential. The question is what is holding YOU back from fulfilling your goals?

---

*Exercise:*

*Write a list of affirmations in the present tense (e.g. 'every day in every way, my life gets better and better'; 'I am a money magnet', etc.).*

*Keep them somewhere handy so you can look at them at least once a day.*

---

www.MillionaireWomenMillionaireYou.com/free

www.MillionaireWomenResources.com

Seema Sharma, Dentist, Entrepreneur, Philanthropist

# How Much Is Enough?

At the age of 43, I have ended up with several strings to my bow, from CEO of Dentabyte Ltd, a dental practice management consultancy, to owner of a state of the art multi-specialist dental centre in the financial district of London Docklands, Smile Impressions Ltd.

I am also a partner in an innovative NHS practice, established after a fierce competitive tendering process, to cater for underprivileged communities in East London, with preventive and outreach dentistry sitting firmly at the centre of its ethos.

Finally, I sit on several committees and steering groups at local and national level, write practice management articles for dental publications, and recently bought a rather sweet family dental practice closer to home.

Small business owners have to balance being 'task oriented' with being 'people oriented' and their greatest challenge is working out how to do this. My formula for success in all my ventures is to surround myself with the right people in the right roles, then to ensure that each business is systems-dependent, not people-dependent. Leadership and management form the bedrock of all my ventures.

One of my latest ventures is my dental practice management consultancy, through which I share my knowledge of running successful dental practices, by training and supporting dentists and their managers. Another is my interest in applying my business entrepreneurial mindset to social entrepreneurship, with the establishment of my charity, The Sharma Foundation.

"Why another venture", you may ask! A tennis coach once told me, that when you get older, you tire of 'doing it' and find it as fulfilling to 'teach it. Make what you will of that!

Go for variety and choice. The secret of success with multiple goals is to train someone to drive the bus, so that when you want to get off, that particular bus route continues to thrive, whilst you set up the next one.

Some ventures are more successful than others – next time you will know to offer the ones that were liked most, but if you don't try, you'll never know.

---

*Exercise:*

*So how much is enough for you? Consider the following when thinking about the concept of enough, and how it applies to your life:*

- *What are the main things that make you happy?*

- *What do you need to thrive?*

- *What do you need to survive at a comfortable level?*

- *What do you have beyond those things needed for survival, comfort, happiness, and thriving?*

- *What do you desire that goes beyond enough — beyond what's needed for survival, comfort, happiness, and thriving? Can you be happy, comfortable and thriving without them?*

- *If you didn't want to have more than enough, could you work less?*

- *If you worked less, could you be happy with enough, and happier doing other things?*

---

www.TheSharmaFoundation.org

www.Dentabyte.co.uk

www.Medibyte.com

www.SmileImpressions.com

Eve Grace-Kelly, Success Coach, Author

# Manage Your Personal Energy

I first came across the concept of Personal Energy Management years ago while developing my Time Management course, and believe that the two systems are really inextricably linked.

Whenever I find myself seemingly suffering from poor Time Management, I immediately look at the level of my Personal Energy Management first and address any imbalance there.

The four elements that have a profound effect on our personal energy are as follows:

Body **+** Emotions **+** Mind **+** Spirit **=** Energy

Find out what your personal energy levels are. For each of the items below, tick ones that apply to you.

| Body | ✓ |
|---|---|
| I don't regularly get at least seven to eight hours of sleep, and I often wake up feeling tired. | |
| I frequently skip breakfast, or I settle for something that isn't nutritious. | |
| I don't work out enough (meaning cardiovascular training at least 3 times a week and strength training at least once a week). | |
| I don't take regular breaks during the day to truly renew and recharge, or I often eat lunch at my desk, if I eat it at all. | |

| Emotions | ✓ |
|---|---|
| I frequently find myself feeling irritable, impatient, or anxious at work, especially when work is demanding. | |
| I don't have enough time with my family and loved ones, and when I'm with them, I'm not always really with them. | |
| I have too little time for the activities that I most deeply enjoy. | |
| I don't stop frequently enough to express my appreciation to others or to savor my accomplishments and blessings. | |

| Mind | ✓ |
|---|---|
| I have difficulty focusing on one thing at a time, and I am easily distracted during the day, especially by email. | |
| I spend much of my day reacting to immediate crises and demands rather than focusing on activities with longer-term value and high leverage. | |
| I don't take enough time for reflection, strategizing, and creative thinking. | |
| I work in the evenings or on weekends, and I almost never take an email-free vacation! | |

| Spirit | ✓ |
|---|---|
| I don't spend enough time at work doing what I do best and enjoy most. | |
| There are significant gaps between what I say is most important to me in my life and how I actually allocate my time and energy. | |
| My decisions at work are more often influenced by external demands than by a strong, clear sense of my own purpose. | |
| I don't invest enough time and energy in making a positive difference to others or to the world. | |

So how did you do? How is your overall energy?

Count up the number of items you ticked above to find out how good you are at managing your personal energy.

| No. | Meaning |
|---|---|
| 0 – 3 | You have excellent energy management skills |
| 4 – 6 | You have reasonable energy management skills |
| 7 – 10 | You have significant energy management deficits |
| 11-16 | It could be that you have a full-fledged energy management crisis! |

If you would like to improve your energy management skills, download our free workbook:

www.QCCGroup.com/energy

*"All the breaks you need in life wait within your imagination. Imagination is the shop of your mind, capable of turning mind energy into accomplishment and wealth."*
Napolean Hill

Janet Beckers, Internet Marketing Expert, Speaker, Author, Mentor

# A Lesson From My Fridge

Our refrigerator in the kitchen is like a giant whiteboard our family uses for special messages. For a long time, it was used to teach our children an important concept. Well, OK, it was also to remind myself of its importance. Here's what was on the fridge...

*A horizontal line.*

**Above the line were the words**: Take responsibility; think of solutions; look for the lessons; keep my power.

**Below the line were the words:** Blame others; make excuses; whinge; victim; give my power away.

Instead of going into lecture mode (very tempting as a parent) every time one of our children would blame other people for their problems, we simply refer to the fridge and concentrate on 'Above The Line Behavior'. My husband and I continuously call each other out about 'Below The Line Behavior.' It's not always easy to accept. I knew the concept had sunk in when I heard my daughter chastising our new puppy for 'Below The Puppy Line Behavior'!

Personal responsibility is the absolute basis of successful behavior. It can be tough acting 'Above The Line'. That's why the majority of us don't do it most of the time. Sure, other people do the wrong thing but it is up to YOU to accept the responsibility for how you will respond. It is up to YOU to decide what behavior you are willing to accept. Up to YOU to challenge yourself to not act like a victim and look at what you DO have the power to do.

---

*Exercise:*

*Be honest with yourself. Do you have excuses for why you haven't created the success you want? For the next 7 days, write down any excuses or blame you find yourself making for why you have not created the success you want.*

*Now turn those excuses in actions for success.....*

---

www.WonderfulWebSeminars.com

*"You cannot change your destination overnight,*
*but you can change your direction overnight."*
Jim Rohn

Glenn Harrold, Hypnotherapist

# Never Stop Learning....

Keep learning and allow yourself to be open to new things.

In my hypnotherapy practice, I once saw an 80-year-old man who had started a degree course and wanted help with recalling information. Total respect!!

I learned a lot from him about being a positive person.

Repeat the following affirmations – they can be repeated silently or out loud.

*"I live my life to the full"*

*"I feel full of optimism for the future"*

www.HypnosisAudio.com

*"The first problem for all of us, men and women,*
*is not to learn, but to unlearn."*
Gloria Steinem

Susanne Jorgensen, Psychologist, Coach, Author

# If You *Couldn't* Fail....

*"Fear seems to be epidemic in our society.*
*We fear beginnings, we fear endings. We fear changing;*
*we fear 'staying stuck'. We fear success; we fear failure.*
*We fear living; we fear dying."*
Susan Jeffers

How often has fear stopped you from getting, having or achieving what you really want? How often have you contemplated doing something new or different only to be overwhelmed by feeling that it's all just too uncomfortable, weird or scary? If so, take heart; it's a normal reaction when you think about stepping outside your 'comfort zone' and stretching yourself.

The problem is when we allow the fear to overcome us and when it keeps us trapped in our comfort zones.

Have you ever played the 'when . . . then' game? I'm sure you know how it goes:

- *When I feel more confident, then I'll go for that promotion*

- *When I feel more confident, then I'll start dating*

- *When I feel more confident, then I'll go for that job.*

Susan Jeffers asserts that what underlies fear is the belief that you hold: "I can't handle it." You don't go for the promotion because you don't think you could handle it if you didn't get it. You don't start dating because you don't think you could handle it if it didn't go well.

Maybe visions of past disasters loom over you or your brain reminds you of some of the terrible mistakes you made in the past. In that moment, all those old feelings overtake you and you become 'paralyzed' and retreat to the safety of your 'comfort zone'.

And so you keep your life on hold, waiting for this thing called 'confidence' to descend upon you in the hope that it will magically change your life and you will be able to do all those things you really want to do.

What you don't realize is that confidence doesn't happen that way. Confidence is a process – it's a process of stepping out of your 'comfort zone' into your 'stretch zone', bit by bit. Every time you do this, your confidence grows. As Susan Jeffers advises, "Feel the fear and do it anyway." It's simple – but not easy!

What might help you though, could be to rethink and reframe what it means to get something 'wrong' or 'fail'.

> *"Failure .... is an attitude, not an outcome."*
> Paul McKenna

Let me tell you a quick story. When I was a little girl – being an 'Army Brat' meant we moved quite a bit. Our move was usually combined with a holiday and one such holiday stands out in my mind. We went to visit a filming studio and actually watched a scene of a film being made. What struck me was how many 'takes' were involved before it was considered a 'wrap up.'

And I'm sure you've seen some television programs or films where, at the end, you get to see the 'takes' that weren't in the final version of the film – they tend to be quite hilarious, actually.

Now, what I find interesting with all this is that these actors do not consider themselves a failure because of a 'mis – take' – or two or three, four or five 'mis-takes.' Do you get where I'm coming from?

Just as in the acting world, in reality, there are many 'takes' in life. A 'mistake' simply means that your current 'take' didn't work. And just like an actor, it simply means having another 'take'.

Life is like a movie of many takes, and if one 'take' doesn't work for you, try another – and another – until you find the 'take' that works. There really is no such thing as failure. Everything is feedback. You get feedback on what works and you get feedback on what doesn't work at this moment in time.

'*Success*' is only feedback about what is working at this moment in time. '*Failure*' is only feedback about what isn't working at this moment in time. So '*failure*' is just a form of feedback. It's what you do with it that really counts.

Your job is to continue making new 'takes' until you get the result you want. You succeed whenever you take the learning from the feedback and apply it to the next 'take'. You only 'fail' if you give up.

---

*Exercise:*

*Think of something you would really like to achieve or something you really want but aren't getting because your fear is getting in the way.*

*Now imagine that I could give you a guarantee that you absolutely could not fail:*

1. *What difference would that make?*

2. *What would you do differently?*

3. *What choices and decisions would you make?*

4. *What would you do next?*

*If that isn't enough, then ask yourself the question: "What would a brave person do?" Then go out and find the tools, resources and mentoring you need – and just do it!*

---

www.TheSinglesGym.com

www.SelectDatingServices.com

*"Don't spend your precious time asking*
*'Why isn't the world a better place?'*
*The question to ask is*
*'How can I make it better?' "*
Leo Buscaglia

# Success Principle #11:
# Learn From Adversity And Defeat

*"Always walk through life as if you have something
new to learn, and you will"*
Vernon Howard

- Occasionally, we all face setbacks. It may just be a minor blip, or it may be a huge obstacle – but much of it depends on the mental attitude with which it is faced.

- Thomas Edison failed many, many times before perfecting the electric light bulb.  He did not see it as failure – just ways in which the electric light bulb wouldn't work!

- Every adversity or defeat also carries with it the seed of an equivalent benefit, which may be a blessing in disguise.

- Learn from the experience and push on towards your goal.

- As Katie Moore says in her Life Lesson: When Things Go Wrong, Don't Go With Them,: "Many relationships and businesses fail because of a lack of understanding. If this is the case, find out why and put things right".

*"Experience is a hard teacher because she gives
the test first, the lesson afterwards."*
Vernon Saunders Law

Nick James, Business Coach, Speaker, Internet Marketer

# Set Your Sights High

When I was still living in Whitley near Reading, UK, I used to walk Keira, my beautiful Alsatian dog every night. Every evening we took the same route - over the motorway, down a country lane and onto a single-track path. I used to stop at the crest of the hill and admire one of the large houses in the landscape. With gold tipped wrought iron gates, manicured lawns and a sweeping driveway, it was simply stunning.

I thought to myself, *"I need to work out what a house like that is worth – so I must start studying the property market immediately."* As part of my research, I went onto a local estate agent's website and, lo and behold, that exact house was for sale!

I seized the opportunity to book a viewing, walked around the house for the first time and instantly fell in love with it. My second viewing was spent visualizing how to put my personal stamp on it and turn it into my own home. Within just one month, I was confident enough to put a firm offer on it.

I visualized living inside this house every night when I walked the dog – this was what I was working towards and it gave me the motivation to achieve each and every day. The first time I had seen my dream house, over the hill, was in March. I moved into it as the proud new owner on 18th September of that same year.

The lesson here is to set your sights high – and don't just dream about things. It's okay to have dreams, but that's the first part. The second part is doing something about it and realizing that, if you're prepared to work for it, your dreams can come true.

www.Nick-James.com

Vinden Grace, Internet Business Specialist/
Digital Coach

# I've Got The T-shirt,
# Now What?

In my line of work, I have been to numerous online business/Internet marketing seminars, bootcamps, workshops, etc., gained a lot of knowledge and then, and this is crucial, applied it.

Over the years, I have come into contact with many people who seem to jump from one 'opportunity' to the next, spending lots of money, but not taking a moment to pause for breath and ask themselves if all of the different pieces of the jigsaw they're constructing will actually fit together. What's happening is that people tend to overlook the crucial need to take a 'helicopter' or strategic view of business opportunities of any description. In other words, they should ask themselves the question: if I buy this or that product or service, how will it fit into my overall business strategy?

The number of people who are setting up their own business is rising at a tremendous rate, but unfortunately, the majority of them fail within the first one or two years. High up on the list of reasons is that the business owner has never set up a business before and does not have a business strategy. In the early stages, I would recommend that any new business owner engage a business mentor.

**Life Lesson**: Firstly, ensure that, whoever you engage as a mentor assists you with developing an overall business strategy. Without this 'destination' in mind, how do you know which 'bus route to take', i.e. which business approach to use or avenue to take?

Secondly, if you want to be successful in your chosen field, associate both with those who have the same aims as you and with leaders in that particular field. Beware of being held back by friends and family who perhaps don't understand your motivation for change or moving on. Subconsciously, they may be holding you back, because they fear a change in your relationship with them.

---

*Exercise:*

*Can you clear define what your business strategy is?*

*If not, why not?*

*What information do you need to enable to develop one?*

*Who can help you in achieving this?*

---

Resources: www.BeginnersInternetGuide.com for beginners in online business; or www.InternetMarketingCoachingOnline.com for intermediates.

*"I expect to pass through life but once. If therefore,
there be any kindness I can show, or any good thing
I can do to any fellow being, let me do it now,
and not defer or neglect it,
as I shall not pass this way again."*
William Penn

Dr Jane Lewis, Career Coach

# Make Your Goals SMART Ones

*"If at first you don't succeed, try and try and try again." (Old proverb)*
*"Do your best and God will do your best."*
(One of my Granny's sayings)

The main distinction between people who are successful and get what they want in life and people who don't, is their attitude.

There's been plenty of psychological research proving what successful people have always known: setting goals increases the likelihood that you will succeed. At the same time, there's a right way to set goals, and goals are generally useless if you don't take action to achieve them.

Just about every management course these days talks about SMART goal setting – that's Specific, Measurable, Actionable, Realistic and Time-bound. You'll come across variants of what the SMART acronym stands for, but most experts agree on the Specific, Measurable and Time-bound.

Specific means clarifying the details. It's not enough to say I want to be happier, or I want to be richer. In what way do you want to be happy, and what do you mean by rich? Goals also need to be stated in the positive. I have had many clients come to me who, when I ask them what they want, keep telling me what they don't want. When you focus on what you don't want, that's where your energy goes, and that tends to be what you get in life.

Measurable is all about *'how will you know when you have it?'* Some while back, I had a goal to attract the ideal partner into my life. I wrote down all the criteria in great detail. I also wrote down what I would be feeling and experiencing when I was with this person. The man who walked into my life didn't meet all the criteria (he's bald, and I had specified full head of hair), but when I am with him, the feelings I have are exactly those I dreamed of. So I know that I have it.

Actionable is concerned with taking the action you need to take in order to achieve your goal. There is a wealth of material that would have you believe that all you need to do is apply mental focus to your goal. However, this ignores two things. Firstly, the very act of taking physical action helps integrate the goal so that everything you do aligns with achieving it. Secondly, most goals require us to get off the couch and do something.

Realistic is pretty much as it sounds. For example, technically, I could enter myself for the next London marathon, get into training and complete it. It's perfectly possible. However, it's extremely unrealistic for me as I hate running, and can find nothing about running a marathon that motivates me.

Time-bound simply means setting a date by when you will have achieved your goal. Day, month and year. As my mother used to say, *"tomorrow never comes"*. Get specific.

Once you set your SMART goals, and decide what actions you need to take to achieve them, you still need to be aware if what you are doing is taking you off track, and be willing to change if needs be. For example, if you had created a financial goal that assumed a buoyant economy, you might need to adjust your goal, and your strategy for achieving it, in the light of a recession.

---

*Exercise:*

- *Set yourself a goal, making it SMART. Ask yourself these questions.*
- *What do I want to achieve? Get specific.*
- *Why?*
- *How will I know when I have it – really get the full picture, including everything you will see, hear, feel and say to yourself when you have it.*
- *Write down your goal – make sure it is positive and time-bound.*

---

www.TheCareerSuccessDoctor.com

Toby Garbett, Olympian

# Toughen Up Your Mental Muscle

I work with children that come from all backgrounds and I have made the transition from funding my own sport through bar work to being a full-time athlete on lottery funding. I have seen a massive transformation in sports science and facilities within my own sport. However, the most important thing that you can't buy is **mental toughness**.

I see youngsters who have all the talent and facilities at their fingertips to do well, but they fail because they don't have the toughness to succeed. If you have mental toughness, you have all you need.

---

*Exercise:*

*You do not have to be born with mental toughness. You learn it through the tasks and challenges life gives you. Here are some strategies for you to gain more mental toughness in everything you do, whether it's in your personal or business life.*

- ***Listen to the experts.** Read biographies and listen to audio programs of winners who have overcome tremendous obstacles and setbacks to become successful.*

- ***Be around successful people**. Hang out with people who have already achieved their goals or who have goals that are similar to yours. If you associate with people who are frustrated by their lack of achievement or who have the same unresolved problems, you will find that you spend your time discussing the negative aspects. Also, some people actually thrive on the attention they get when they feel bad! If you belong to a strong community of like-minded people, you will be motivated and have a strong sense of purpose for succeeding. You are also likely to get the right kind of support you need.*

- ***Adopt 'What next?' thinking**. When something goes wrong, don't dwell on it. Work out what you are going to do to set it right. Move forward; find an answer. Keeping a journal will really help. Writing down your accomplishments – what went well – what could be improved – what progress have you made towards your goal – whether you are focused or easily strayed onto other activities.*

- ***Focus on your desired results.** Do what's necessary now and stay in the present. By not worrying about what happened yesterday or what is going to happen tomorrow, two-thirds of your worries simply disappear!*

- ***Step outside your comfort zone.** Do something different, or in a different way, every day. This might be taking a different route to work, shopping in a different store, reading instead of watching TV for relaxation. This will help you to be better prepared to handle diverse environments with greater calm and confidence. Make a note in your journal about the impact this has on you and your mindset.*

- ***Expect the unexpected.** Although you can't control what nature and others do, you can anticipate what may happen, and prepare as best you can. Importantly, you can also control your response to what happens.*

---

www.TobyGarbett.com

*"You see things; and you say, 'Why?'*
*But I dream things that never were;*
*and I say, 'Why not?' "*
George Bernard Shaw

Marie O'Riordan, Communications Excellence
Specialist

# The Art Of Sharing

I didn't have to be a Communications Expert to realize that one of the most effective ways to bond with people is to eat with them. What enhances your key relationships with people even more is your ability to share and care, not just with food, but your thoughts, experiences and encouraging words too.

Please repeat with me...

*"I make a conscious effort to share and care more with the people in my life on a daily basis from now on."*

My diet is nut free as nuts and nut oils give me ferociously intense migraine. I discovered this the hard way some years ago after being rushed to an emergency room by ambulance after eating cashews and pistachios! I also live caffeine free for the same reason. Also listen to your body and it will tell you so much.

---

*Exercise:*

*In this frenetic world, we don't always find the time to bond with people, whether they are a new co-worker, neighbor, or team-mate, etc. But it's vital if you hope to have an enjoyable and lasting relationship with these people. Follow these strategies to enhance your relationships.*

*Find out as much as you can about the other person. Ask lots of questions during your first conversations with them. Really focus on them. Look for any common ground in your backgrounds, education, work or family histories. People love to be listened to and friends will feel closer to you. They will turn to you if they feel you're paying attention and offering sound advice about their problems.*

*Discover some favorite music, artist or movie that you both like. Go and see movies together, attend concerts or go to book signings together.*

*Go out to dinner or shopping together, or even a nice walk. These are ideal activities to break the ice, and you may discover that you've got similar likes and dislikes.*

*Finally, remember what drew you to your existing close friends and colleagues and apply some of those bonding ideas to this relationship.*

---

www.MarieORiordanInternational.com

*"Take hold of your own life.*
*See that the whole existence is celebrating.*
*These trees are not serious, these birds are not serious.*
*The rivers and the oceans are wild, and everywhere there is fun,*
*everywhere there is joy and delight. Watch existence,*
*listen to existence and become part of it."*
Osho

Amanda van der Gulik, Entrepreneur,
Coach for Kids

# Hard 'n' Crumbly On The Outside, Warm 'n' Sweet On The Inside!

In my life, I've often found that the people who have the toughest protective shells on the outside are often warm and sweet on the inside. These people can sometimes hurt your feelings without even realizing it. They are simply trying to protect themselves from their own past experiences.

So try not to take it personally. Although, it may not be easy, it's so worth it to just stay positive and realize that their hurtful words actually have nothing whatsoever to do with you.

I heard a saying once that has stuck with me and helped me in many a situation. *"What they think is NONE of your business... What you think is NONE of their business!"* **Anon.**

So keep this in mind the next time someone says something or does something to hurt you. It's most likely not even about you. Have patience, just listen, and see it as a possible mirror. Take the lesson if it is yours to receive. If not, then just see it as their own mirrored lesson.

Don't take it personally. You may just discover that underneath that Hard 'n Crumbly exterior, there is a Warm 'n Sweet soul inside that's been hurt and needs a little patience and a little love.

If that person remains negative around you, then simply choose not to be around them. It's not as hard as that may seem. Even if you cannot escape them physically, you always have the opportunity to escape them mentally.

See the situation from outside yourself. It'll seem so much easier to handle. Always try to find the Warm 'n' Sweet!

www.TeachingChildrenAboutMoney.com

Seema Sharma, Dentist, Entrepreneur, Philanthropist

# Take The Opportunity To Give Back

We are all at a different stage in our journey. Some are starting out, some are nearing retirement. The icing on the cake has to be the opportunity to try something that you did not in your wildest dreams think you had the time or resource for. After participating in '*Slumdog Secret Millionaire*', despite being busy with work and having adolescent children, I established a new charity, The Sharma Foundation, to help underprivileged communities in India and in East London.

Volunteering in the slums of Mumbai, I despaired at the sheer magnitude of the poverty and deprivation I saw, but marveled at the energy and determination of slum dwellers striving to better their lives. I was humbled by the amazing work of hundreds of grassroots charity organizations. The sheer scale of the population, cost of living, lack of education and skills shortages felt insurmountable, but I felt that doing nothing was not an option.

My personal compass had been reset and a new bus journey beckoned. The bus I wanted to be on was the bus that took education to the streets of Mumbai to educate the thousands of street children whose families had moved from villages to cities, in search of opportunities. This, after all, was the same economic migration pattern that had led my great grandparents to set sail for western coasts and look at what a successful journey that was for me!

If you like to join me on the journey of social entrepreneurship, either now or someday, subscribe to my newsletter at www.TheSharmaFoundation.org

www.Dentabyte.co.uk

www.Medibyte.com

www.SmileImpressions.com

# Success Principle #12:
# Maintain Sound Physical
# And Mental Health

- Complete Curly Martin's exercise in her Life Lesson: **Coach Yourself To Health**. As Curly says, *"Once you understand what it means to you to be healthy, you can now decide what changes you may need to organize to ensure your continuing health"*.

- Exercise produces both physical and mental resilience. It clears sluggishness and dullness from both the mind and body. In other words, take an holistic view – what affects your physical health also affects your mental health.

- If you do not have the willpower to keep yourself in good physical condition, then you lack the power of will to maintain a positive mental attitude towards other important circumstances that control your life.

- A positive mental attitude is the most important quality for sound physical and mental health (see Success Principle #1).

- When we are happy, we are not prone to physical and mental anxieties. Being happy releases endorphins, thereby making you feel good– to be happy, make someone else happy! But as Susanne Jorgensen says, in her Life Lesson: **Relationship Success From The Inside Out,** *"The way to find love is to become so much yourself [i.e. be authentic and true to yourself], that you attract others of your own kind..."*

- Maintain an attitude of gratitude. Refuse to grumble or complain when circumstances look difficult. Be grateful for where you are now, and for where you are headed. Look around for things to be grateful for. You'll be surprised to find quite a few.

Stephanie Hale, Publishing Expert and
Writing Coach

# Take 12 Seconds

Now here's an interesting thing. Millionaires take 12 seconds longer
on average than most people before making a decision to buy
something. This is because they understand the value of money and
are more likely to weigh up the pros and cons before making any
purchase.

Here's something else that's interesting. The majority of people don't
know what their income and expenditure is. They ask money experts
for help with their finances thinking that the solution is going to be
terribly complicated. Yet, often the answer is as simple as knowing
where their money is going each month.

It's all too easy to get caught in the trap where every penny you earn
gets spent. You can spot the big spend each month – like a new boiler
or car repairs. What might be causing just as much of a headache
might be the smaller purchases such as chocolate bars, magazines or
toiletries that all add up over the space of a year. The fact is you don't
have to spend all the money that you earn. A generally accepted rule
of thumb is that you should aim to save and invest at least 10% of
your income.

Most millionaires know exactly how much money is coming in and
flowing out – both personal and business. Often they developed this
skill when they were broke and the habit stayed with them. They
know that to truly achieve financial freedom, you must keep track of
your income and expenditure.

If you don't already know what your incomings and outgoings are
– either in your home or business - then you need to get a clearer
picture. Are you spending money on necessities or luxuries, for
example? Just the simple act of writing this down will help you feel
more in control of your finances. You might even be surprised to
discover that if you eliminate something small from your life or reduce

its frequency (like bottled drinks or ready-made sandwiches), you can drastically reduce your expenditure.

---

*Exercise:*

*Make a log of your income and expenditure for the next month. Record each item meticulously, no matter how big or small. Understand exactly where your money is going, to the penny. Identify what are necessities and what are luxuries.*

*Now here's an inspiring fact. Did you know that if you saved approximately £13 every week over the course of your working life, that with compounding, you would retire with £1.2 million in the bank? Think of the potential in that statement if you started saving and investing that money for your children right now!*

---

www.MillionaireWomenMillionaireYou.com/free

www.MillionaireWomenResources.com

*"It is your responsibility to see that your life works out the way you want it. No one else can do it for you. The power to change your life is within you."*
Heidi Baer

Susanne Jorgensen, Psychologist, Coach, Author

# If You Believe...

*"Whether you believe you can or you believe
you can't, you are right."*
Henry Ford

Your world is a hologram that is reflecting back to you whatever you believe. Your relationships, too, are a mirror of your beliefs about relationships.

- If you believe that most people are out to get you, that's going to be your dominant experience.

- If you believe that men aren't trustworthy, that's what you are most likely to experience.

- If you believe that all women are after your money, then that's what you'll get.

- If you believe money is hard to get or you have to work really hard for money, you're going to have to work really hard for very little money.

- If you predict things won't work out for you in the future because they haven't worked out for you in the past - then that will be your experience.

- If you believe you aren't worthy or deserving of a happy relationship – you won't have a happy relationship.

- If you believe you are unlovable – love will elude you.

If you hold these kinds of beliefs, you will find that history will keep repeating itself. You see, the same experiences are repeated because the same thoughts, the same beliefs, actions and behaviors are replicated each time.

Do you find that you sabotage what could be potentially good relationships or do you find that you sabotage your success in other areas of your life? If you recognize this, your life is being driven by some powerful limiting beliefs. Whether you call this phenomenon the 'law of attraction' or 'expectancy theory' or 'self-fulfilling prophecy', the bottom line is that your beliefs drive your behaviors.

If you look at your relationship history, are you aware of certain patterns? Maybe you keep attracting the same type of person. Maybe you keep attracting the wrong kind of person. Maybe your relationships keep ending the same way or for the same reasons. If that's the case, your life is being driven by some unconscious limiting *beliefs* – which simply means, beliefs which you are not aware of.

> *The problem with your life isn't your life –*
> *the problem lies with your beliefs*

I remember years ago attending a Tony Robbins three day seminar in London. One of the days culminated in a 'fire-walk.' We spent some time getting into the right 'state' and working on any beliefs that might sabotage us achieving this goal.

I was all psyched up. I knew I could do it. I was ready to go . . . . and then it happened. As I stood in front of the fire walk ready to step on the coals, the helpers jumped in front of me and started stirring the coals around. What looked like lumps of black coal before had now turned into red glowing hot coals. I froze. In that moment, I wasn't sure I could do it without burning my feet.

When I share that story with people, some of them proceed to tell me how the whole experience is 'rigged' and how anyone can actually do the fire walk. Now, while they might be right – they are missing the point completely. Even if it's 'rigged' and anyone, therefore, can do the fire walk, when you are standing there in front of the coals – what you believe as you stand there in that split second of time - not the cold hard facts - determines whether you will actually take that walk across the coals. Your beliefs – not the facts – drive your behaviors.

We are all capable of so much in life but few of us have reached, or will ever reach, our full potential because our beliefs about what we can have, do, and achieve get in our way. The good news is that you can change your beliefs. You can choose to take on life-enhancing beliefs rather than continue to live out your limiting beliefs. Taking the first step involves becoming more aware of what your limiting beliefs are.

---

*Exercise:*

*1. What are some beliefs you have about your future?*

*2. What are some beliefs you have about your future relationships?*

*If you aren't sure what your beliefs are, for each question, work backwards. Think about what keeps happening in your life and relationships and ask yourself - "To get that outcome, what beliefs must I be holding?"*

*Now think about what beliefs you would prefer to have.*

*1. What would you like to believe about your future?*

*2. What would you like to believe about a future relationship?*

*Step into that belief and imagine what it feels like to really believe it.*

*1. Imagine what would be different for you.*

*2. Imagine what you would be doing that you aren't doing.*

*3. Imagine what you would be doing more of or less of.*

*And imagine if you were making those changes, what would happen.*

*When beliefs change, so do behaviors. When your behaviors change, so do the responses of people around you and when the responses of others change, your experiences of others and the world changes.*

www.TheSinglesGym.com

www.SelectDatingServices.com

Dr Jane Lewis, Career Coach

# Take Time For Friends And Family

*"God gave us memories so we can have roses in winter"* – old saying.

When we're rushing around and trying to juggle several balls in the air at once, it's really easy to lose touch with friends and family. Even your immediate family.

Yet, putting time aside to do something enjoyable together is so precious. It could be as simple as meeting up for a coffee, or lunch, or getting on Skype™, or going for a walk together, helping your mum in her garden – or have her help you in yours! Flying kites from a nearby hill, cooking together...the possibilities are endless.

My mother has dementia, and it's made me realize two things:

- Firstly, how important friends and family are when you are old

- Secondly, the wonder of treasuring happy times together - both in the moment, and as memories later on.

---

*Exercise:*

*Imagine yourself sitting on a rocking chair in your old age, and reflecting back on your life, in particular on the times that you have had with your friends and family.*

*Are you smiling at the wonderful times you have had together? Or are you thinking that you were rushing around so much trying to be the perfect employee, the perfect boss, etc., that you often had to cancel time with people that really matter to you.*

*If the latter, what can you do to address the imbalance?*

*Why not make a list of those people who have touched your heart and who you would like to spend more time with. Then contact them, pick up the phone and have a chat, arrange that lunch or coffee, go for that walk – reconnect!*

---

www.TheCareerSuccessDoctor.com

Eve Grace-Kelly, Success Coach, Author

# Do You Brighten Up A Room When You Enter….. Or When You Leave?

We spend so much time on building up our knowledge to ensure that, when we are interviewed for a new job, our intelligence shines through, that we sometimes forget even more important aspects of the interaction. Whether the interviewer feels we would be a good fit for the organization. That we can be liked by our future colleagues. That we can also be trusted and valued.

For a few years now, the universities have been turning out well-educated, bright people, some of whom have a big problem in finding suitable employment. There is so much competition for every job in the country. Career coaching is, therefore, 'hot' right now. After a few months of being rejected at the interview stage, people are realizing that they could benefit from some coaching – not on how to gain more knowledge, but on how to 'wow' their potential employer.

But it's not just limited to getting that job you want. The ability to brighten up a room when you enter affects many different aspects of our lives. In our careers – what is it that people notice about us to recommend us for a promotion? Or what is it that makes people sit up and take notice when we want to put our opinion forward in a meeting? In our relationships – what is it that people notice about us when we enter the room that immediately, they want to get to know us?

So if you were asked, "**Do you brighten up a room when you enter….. or when you leave?**" – what would your answer be? Even more revealing, how would other people answer that question?

If you run your own business, what would your clients say to their contacts – contacts that could become your future clients? Personal recommendations are the most flattering and the most lucrative. They are also likely to be the most loyal customers, coming back with repeat business, because they prefer to stick with who they know (provided, of course, that they receive good service) rather than look for a different supplier. If they do need to engage a new supplier, they are much more likely to speak to other trusted business owners who they use.

So how can you improve your ability to be the person who people recommend for that new job; who people recommend as a supplier; or who people recommend to get to know on a social level?

The simple answer is to get to know them as a person, not just as a job title. Build rapport with them. Gain their trust. This can be done with everyone in both business and personal scenarios.

---

*Exercise:*

*Make a list of who you need to know (both in your business and personal lives). So, include your clients, colleagues, managers, suppliers.*

*Then decide to do something about getting to know them, and to let them get to know you. Be of real value to them.*

*Here are some tips:*

*DO...*

- *Grow your business and personal networks by meeting new people. Attend more industry or business events, and participate in social groups. This can be a bit daunting at first, and you may be going outside your comfort zone, but have in mind that the majority of others there could very well be feeling the same as you.*

- *Decide how many people you want to meet and get connected with at the event. To build up your confidence, you may decide that, for the first couple of events, this will only be one new connection. As your confidence and success grows, raise this number.*

- *Listen more carefully to others' names so that you remember them. If you didn't hear their name, ask them. They will be more flattered that you really want to get to know them. Say their name when you get the opportunity to in a conversation so that you are more likely to remember it. Be careful not to overdo it though!*

- *Stand up and walk around. You will be noticed more than if you were sitting in a corner waiting for someone to come and talk with you.*

- *Focus on finding how you can be of value to others. This will help to build your relationship with them. Offer some kind of opportunity – referrals, recommendation, or information, without looking for a return favor. This will build trust.*

- *Ask lots of 'open' questions to find out about the person, their business, and what they are looking for.*

- *Make sure that you follow up on any promises you make. This is an area that many people forget.*

- *Re-connect with three or four people every day who you may not have spoken to in a while.*

*DON'T...*

- *Get your business card out at every opportunity. People like to get to know you first. It also smacks of desperation!*

- *Forget to ask for a delegate list in advance of attending an event. This will help you identify specific people you want to meet.*

- *Contact other people only when you want something - people notice.*

- *Say you'll attend something and then forget or change your mind about going.*

- *Dismiss someone's spouse, assistant, secretary, or a waiter, the mail delivery person or a security guard! These are all important people who can sometimes have a big influence on someone or be the 'gatekeeper' to someone you want to get to know. Get to know them as people.*

---

www.QCCGroup.com

Janet Beckers, Internet Marketing Expert,
Speaker, Author, Mentor

# Treat Your Bitter Lemons With Respect

I love the tangy sweetness of lemon cake. The thought of boiling lemons and then pureeing them whole sounds horrible. You would expect it to be bitter and pithy. But handling a bitter lemon with the right care results in a cake that is unique and full of flavor.

This is really an analogy for handling difficult customers in your business. People who complain, seem to expect unreasonable service or approach your business with suspicion because of bad experiences they have had with similar businesses. They are the customers that really test your tolerance and patience.

It's very tempting to take their aggression personally and dismiss or even argue with them. Instead, I see them as a gift. I know if I take their criticism as suggestions for improvement rather than as a personal insult, my business will become stronger. If I thank them for their feedback and treat them with respect, I will earn their respect in return. After all, they cared enough to let me know.

Without fail, when I am genuinely grateful to a 'lemon', they respond with surprise and gratitude. They are used to being ignored or criticized in return and more often than not then become a very loyal customer.  So by treating the 'bitter lemons' in your business with the right care and respect, they may very well become something special you want to share with your friends (a.k.a. your other customers).

---

*Exercise:*

*Visualize customers and friends who you think have acted like bitter lemons at some time.*

*Write down 3 reasons to be grateful for them and how you can change the way you deal with them.*

---

www.WonderfulWebSolutions.com

Vinden Grace, Internet Business Specialist/
Digital Coach

# It's All In The Mind....

Much of the personal development literature contains research on the effects of our thoughts on our motivation, our actions and so on. Our thoughts can even affect our health! A positive mental attitude has been advocated for decades, but it's worth reminding ourselves just how influential this can be, in our working lives, sporting endeavors and our personal relationships (e.g. dare we approach the gorgeous object of our attention?). Determination can go a long way towards success while self-belief gives you confidence and focus. Your thoughts can and will create your perception of reality. So ensure that those thoughts are ones that you truly want!

"If you think you are beaten, you are.
If you think you dare not, you won't.
If you like to win, but don't think you can,
It's almost a cinch that you won't.

If you think you'll lose, you've lost,
For in our world you'll find
Success begins with a person's will.
It's all in the state of mind.

If you think you're out-classed, you are;
You've got to think high to rise.
You've got to be very sure of yourself
Before you can win the prize.

Life's battles don't always go
To the strongest or fastest man.
But sooner or later the person who wins
Is the person who thinks she can."

Walter D. Wintle

---

*Exercise:*

*Recognizing where we use negative patterns can help us to stop using those patterns, thereby weakening them.*

*So, keep a notepad handy and keep a record of your words and thoughts. Which are positive and which are negative?*

*Don't beat yourself up about negative self-talk: we all do it from time to time! Just be aware of the difference in the energies between the positive and negative thoughts and their influence on you.*

---

www.QCCGroup.com

*"Do not follow where the path may lead.*
*Go instead where there is no path and leave a trail."*
George Bernard Shaw

Kathleen Ronald, Networker, Speaker, Trainer, Consultant

# All Things Are Possible…

*"Through God ALL things are possible!"*
Matthew 19:26

Reflecting on the hundreds of lessons from my life, I wondered, *"Which is THE ONE that serves me at a 'core' level, in all areas of my life?"*

**Through God ALL things are possible!**…this verse has served me thousands of times in my life.

My mother, Bunny, was the catalyst for this lesson. A devout Catholic with six kids, she was in church and praying six days a week most of her life. Her #1 goal was getting those six kids into heaven. Like most kids do, I showed up and pretended to be involved. My parents always wanted me to be a nun and I secretly prayed to not be called. Then of course, imagining it to be a sin to not be open to the call, I spent time in the confessional seeking God's forgiveness.

I always admired and wondered how people found their faith, grew it and used it on a daily basis. After my Mom transitioned almost 18 years ago, I began meditating and considering the lesson 'through God, ALL things are possible!' Whenever my faith seemed weak, this phrase would instantly remind me that my human thinking, my limited faith, were all that stood between me and a miracle. Think about it… it doesn't say all things are possible if you are Catholic, or if it is Sunday, or if you've been good, or if God is in the mood. It says…ALL things are possible.

It is the greatest gift my mother shared by her living example. Through it, my faith expanded to levels I never dreamed of. I've been blessed to be so connected and to witness so many miracles. Not only is my faith stronger, it is my source of strength, encouragement, hope, love, and support. Going beyond scripture, it fuels my soul. It is the foundation for how to live my life! It goes beyond my faith in God. Because of my faith, I now have faith in who I am and what I am here to do! Lacking faith in yourself is a tragedy that withholds your gifts and talents from the world. Meditate on this lesson. It will also serve you to explore, expand and illuminate your faith. It is your source of healing for yourself and the world around you. I promise! Faith up!

---

*Exercise:*

*Do you have a faith? How much is your faith muscle being exercised? On a scale of 1-10 with 10 being the high score, how would you score the level of faith you have in you?*

*What could you do in 10 minutes a day to build your faith?*

---

www.Speaktacular.com

*"If you obey all the rules, you miss all the fun."*
Katharine Hepburn

# Success Principle #12½:
# Be In The Know

- As Emma Tiebens states in her Life Lesson: **Invest In YOU, Inc.....,** investing in your own personal growth, *"will take you places you've never been before, unlock doors you wouldn't have otherwise seen and connect with people you wouldn't have met before!"*

- Find out everything you can about what you want to achieve or succeed in.

- Read relevant books.

- Listen to appropriate audios.

- Talk to experts in your chosen fields.

- Do whatever it takes to improve your knowledge. This will prove invaluable in helping you make wise decisions.

- As Paul Avins says in his Life Lesson: **If You Want To Earn More You Must Learn More**, *"I keep investing in books, CDs and training courses.... even when others close to me thought I was crazy and could not afford it. My mindset was that I couldn't afford NOT to invest in me - as clearly I didn't know the right information to get the results I wanted".*

- Improved knowledge will also help you maintain confidence as you progress towards achieving your goal.

- Be wary, though, of developing the art of procrastination. It's easy to get stuck in 'research mode' and become a perpetual student, never taking any actions. Follow the Pareto optimality principle or 80/20 Rule - see Eve Grace-Kelly's Life Lesson: **The 80/20 Rule – Use Your Time Wisely.**

- Gain some knowledge from experts, then practice applying it. See what works for you and do more of that and less of what doesn't work. Then acquire some more knowledge in your chosen field and Lather, Rinse, Repeat! Improvement in anything is an iterative process – congratulate yourself on your accomplishments as you take each step. Here's to your success!

*"To know that we know what we know, and that we do not know what we do not know, that is true knowledge."*
Henry David Thoreau

Amanda van der Gulik, Entrepreneur, Coach for Kids

# You Can Have Your Cake AND Eat It Too!

How often have you been told that you need to struggle in order to survive? In order to thrive?

Maybe you were a little girl who was constantly told that it hurts to be beautiful? Or maybe you were a little boy who was told to just be brave, or tough it out, that boys don't cry?

Well, who came up with those awful rules, anyway?

*I say you can have your cake AND eat it too!*

It's all in the way you choose to think about your life. Do you always see it as a constant struggle? Is life hard?

Why not choose to believe that it's easy? Would it really hurt to decide that, from this moment onwards, your life is great?

You know, often, pessimistic people will tell optimistic people that their ideas, their dreams, are NOT realistic? Have you been told that? I have! Many times!

And yet, no matter how awful life can sometimes get for me, I am still always perceived to be the girl who gets what she wants. Who is always happy.

Am I? Of course not. I have awful moments too. I also have terrible things that happen to me. Without them, I wouldn't be who I am today. But, you know what? I choose to look for the light. To find the positive lesson in every life lesson thrown my way.

I choose to believe that I can have my cake AND eat it too! Why not?

If you work diligently and determinedly at something, then don't you feel that you deserve your just desserts?

Of course you do! Don't let anyone else EVER take your cake away from you. It's yours! Of course, you can always choose to share!

Have your cake AND eat it too! Life's a party, if only you choose it to be!

www.FunCakeDecoratingIdeas.com

Andy Harrington, Peak Performance Specialist

# How To Have A Life Of Fewer Problems

*"Make your goals so big, so inspiring, so compelling that they make your problems seem insignificant by comparison"*
Andy Harrington

By the age of 30, I had accomplished nothing. I was in a boring repetitive job for Churchill, providing motor insurance quotes all day long. My first marriage had failed after just a few months, and I was addicted to class A drugs. I was broke, living alone in a cold damp bedsit and my life was slowly going nowhere. A friend of mine had left Churchill just a few months previously, and we got talking about the idea of starting a business of our own. We didn't have any money to start the business, but we did have a plan to pull in £1.2 Million in our first year!

I was excited, and for the first time in far too long, focused. I began to forget about my problems and my current situation in life and started to dream about what life would be like if we could pull it off. I went to several business banks with our cash flow projections, full of enthusiasm. They asked me a few questions about my background, and quickly decided this was a far-fetched business. They politely showed me where the door was.

But my goal was too big to let it die so easily, so I changed my approach and told the next bank I wanted to borrow some money to buy a car. It's odd; they wouldn't lend me money to grow an asset, but were more than happy to lend me money to buy a liability! So, we got the business started with a £10,000 'car loan', and today, that business has now pulled in more than £46,000,000!

In life, I have discovered that you get one of two things: either you have problems, or you have goals, but you'll never have neither. You see, the mind can't live in a vacuum; it has to have something to focus on. So, in the absence of goals that inspire you to move yourself, you get problems that demand you move instead. I learned that the reason I didn't have the life I deserved was not because I was lazy, but because my goals were just not big enough to inspire me.

---

*Exercise:*

*What is your dream way of making money, regardless of your current life conditions?*

*What is the first step you can take to make this happen? And when will you take this step?*

*What is the second step ........ You get the idea!*

---

www.PowerToAchieve.co.uk/freedvd

*"The best day of your life is the one on which you decide your life is your own. No apologies or excuses. No one to lean on, rely on or blame. The gift is yours - it is an amazing journey - you alone are responsible for the quality of it. This is the day your life really begins."*
Bob Moawad, Author & Speaker

Toby Garbett, Olympian

# Develop A Sense Of Personal Power

Throughout the life lessons in this or any other book, none of it is possible without the belief in your own ability.  This became very apparent to me at the age of 19 whilst on the river overtaking Matthew Pinsent (4-time Olympic champion) in a single scull and I had the realization of self-belief.

This was a fantastic moment, but was also two-sided in the fact that I wish I had had self-belief from an earlier age.

Who knows what we could all achieve?

---

*Exercise:*

*There are many things that you can do to raise your self-esteem; too many to include here, but one fun exercise you can do is to* **Toot Your Horn!**

*This exercise will boost your confidence through exploring and identifying what makes you feel good. Then by regularly reminding yourself of these, new brain pathways will be created and your 'self-esteem muscle' will be strengthened.*

*On a blank piece of paper, write answers to the following statements:*

*1. I like myself because:*

*2. I feel good about:*

*3. I'm an expert at:*

*4. My friends would tell you I have a great:*

*5. Add any other statements of your own (or ask someone you trust for additional statements):*

*Boost your self-esteem daily by reading your Toot Your Horn worksheet. It will remind you of your natural resources and personal power.*

---

Eve Grace-Kelly, Success Coach, Author

# Blast Those Obstacles!

*"Others can stop you temporarily —*
*you are the only one who can do it permanently."*
Zig Ziglar

What do you do when you are faced with an obstacle, a decision you need to make, a problem you need to solve? Are you one of those people who quickly comes up with a solution and then regrets it? Or do you take your time, taking everything into consideration before you decide on the solution?

To be honest, there isn't a right decision here. There are pros and cons to both approaches. The key point is whether you are afraid to even tackle the many obstacles that confront you on a day-to-day basis.

For me, I used to prefer to take my time, weigh up all the odds and then decide. Probably because, at heart, I'm a 'people pleaser'. I like to ensure that everyone is happy. In my work environment, I used to canvass everyone's opinion and secretly pray that everyone was of the same opinion! If they weren't, I'd start to feel out of my depth in my ability to make the right decision..... and therein lies the rub. I always wanted to make the RIGHT decision. I hated being wrong.

And that's probably still my preferred approach, but throughout my career, I have been pushed, or even taken the initiative, to step outside my comfort zone and have had to make fast decisions. It's definitely an acquired taste!

Whether we are faced with a problem, a big decision, or even deciding something small such as what to eat for dinner, we go through a sequence of events.

All successful people are solution-oriented, and they go through the same process:

1) They clearly define the problem

2) They assess what is holding them back from achieving their goal

3) They determine all the possible solutions – all the potential things they could do to overcome whatever obstacle is in the way of achieving their goal

4) They take action – they decide which solution is the best one and then go for it!

Sometimes this process can take a long time; other times it's instantaneous – it's something we do day in, day out.

www.QCCGroup.com

*"What is the difference between an obstacle and an opportunity? Our attitude towards it. Every opportunity has a difficulty, and every difficulty has an opportunity."*
J. Sidlow Baxter

# Afterword

## Make it happen

*"No one else can sing your song, write your story or dance your dance; you are the designer of your own destiny!"*
Buddha

## Measure your success

This book contains a number of exercises that, if you do them with a positive intent, will start to make the change that you want in your life, your career, and your business. You will start to change your mindset with regard to just how successful you can be.

Visit www.QCCGroup.com/wheeloflife to find out how happy or fulfilled you are at this point in time. Then reflect on the Life Lessons in this book, work through the exercises, make the necessary changes in your life and then recalibrate where you are on the Wheel of Life by revisiting the website.

Take a moment to look back at your life over the last week and ask yourself the following questions:

On a scale of 0 – 10, where 0 = not at all and 10 = maximum possible:

1) How happy was I as I went about my day?

2) How centered or balanced was I overall?

3) How powerfully did I move toward creating my ideal life?

Now, ask yourself:

1) What could I do to improve the answers to each of the above questions by just one point?

2) What actions am I willing to commit to this week to improve my score?

3) When will I carry out these actions?

Anthony Robbins is credited as having once said something along the lines of, *"If you always do what you've done, you'll always get what you've always got"*.

Well, even if we make a small change in our lives, and do it consistently, over time, our actions will yield great results.

As Lao Tzu said, *"A journey of a thousand miles, starts with a single step."*

What can you do to step outside your 'comfort zone' and do something different today, and then tomorrow, and the day after that? Once you start, the momentum will build upon itself......

Have a fabulous life – we'd love to hear about YOUR life lessons, and these may feature in future books in this series.

- How did the life lessons in this book impact your life?

- What insights did you gain?

- What actions were you inspired to take?

- What results did you have?

Come and share your results in our community at www.UltimateLifeLessonsClub.com

# Meet The Contributors

**Eve Grace-Kelly** CWC MBILD MAPM MISMA is *"one of the UK's leading Success Coaches"* (Jonathan Jay, founder of The Coaching Academy), and is CEO and co-founder of Quantum Coaching and Consulting Group (a leading Personal and Business Success Coaching, Consulting, Training and Wellness organization). She has wide-ranging experience of setting up and running businesses including a recruitment company, a management consultancy, Internet businesses, a personal and business success coaching company and even a gym! She has decades of success in Project and Programme Management Consultancy and Performance Coaching for major, leading clients. Corporate clients include Lloyds Bank, Legal and General Insurance, Fidelity Investments, NatWest Life, WH Smith, the NHS, J Sainsbury's, Her Majesty's Revenue and Customs, KPMG, Glaxo SmithKline, National Power, NASA, 3UK, the European Commission in Brussels, and the pan-European aviation organization, EUROCONTROL. Eve is a qualified and experienced Success Coach, Personal Coach and Business Coach. In addition to her qualifications as a Weight-Management consultant, she is also a Certified Wellness Coach. She is also certified in Neuro-Linguistic Programming (NLP) and Stress Management. Pursuing her constant interest in personal development, Eve has achieved Member status of the British Institute for Learning and Development. She's also a certified Work-Life Balance consultant and endeavors to follow her own advice in this regard, but admits that she doesn't always succeed! As a member of the European Mentoring and Coaching Council, she upholds high standards in ethics and integrity in all she does. Eve divides her time between England, Belgium and America. www.QCCGroup.com www.EveGraceKelly.com

**Vinden Grace** M Sc B Sc (Hons) MIoD F IDM CWC MBILD MISMA is a long-established Internet Business Specialist/Digital Coach, with a first degree from Warwick University Business School and a Master's degree in computing from Boston University. He is a founding Director of Quantum Coaching and Consulting Group (a leading Personal and Business Success Coaching, Consulting, Training and Wellness organization). Vinden has extensive experience of setting up and running online and offline businesses including a recruitment company, a management consultancy, Internet businesses and a personal and business coaching company. Many years of Project Management and Planning Consultancy for blue-chip clients, such as Deutsche Bank, the UK government and the European Commission, have given him the background to initiate and complete a variety of successful projects. Vinden is a qualified and experienced Life or Personal Coach, Business Coach and a Certified Guerrilla Information Marketer®. He is also certified in Wellness Coaching, Neuro-Linguistic Programming (NLP) and Stress Management. Reflecting his lifelong interest in personal development, Vinden has achieved Member status of the British Institute for Learning and Development. Finally, he's a long-time member of the UK's top organization for business leaders, the Institute of Directors, and, in 2010, was elected a Fellow of the Institute of Direct Marketing. Vinden is married to Eve Grace-Kelly and also divides his time between England, Belgium and America. www.QCCGroup.com www.VindenGrace.com

**Tracy Repchuk** is the #1 Woman in the world for Internet marketing, an international speaker and motivator, and appears on the world's largest stages educating and mentoring on *How to Turn Your Passion Into Profits*. She has been an entrepreneur since 1985, and lives the freedom lifestyle with her husband and 3 children - who often accompany her. She is the bestselling author of *31 Days to Millionaire Marketing Miracles*, a book that has over 115 online testimonials and is being praised as the Internet Marketing Go To Guide for the Industry. Tracy specializes in Internet marketing campaigns that build a cohesive corporate or personal brand using an integrated web strategy that produces automated streams of income and continuous traffic and prospects. With over 10,000 loyal members world-wide, she provides environments and information to every level from Internet marketing newbie to entrepreneurial millionaires. In addition, she has appeared on TV: ABC7, King5, 7 For Your Money, 4 On Your Side, WBZ, Report on Business Television, CTV news, USA Today, radio, magazine, newspapers and her work has appeared in over 50 publications. She has won New Internet Marketing Success of the year, Stevie Award Finalist for Mentor of the Year, International Women's Day Feminine Leader, Canadian Entrepreneur of the Year nominee, Chamber of

Commerce Business Woman of the Year nominee and Who's Who of IT Professionals, Who's Who of Professionals, Who's Who of Entrepreneurs and Who's Who of Presidents. Tracy focuses on balance and teaching others how to build an online business so you can make money while you sleep. She has thousands of clients around the world, and is getting called the Robert Kyosaki of Internet Marketing. If you want to turn your Passion into Profits - Get your free report at: www.MillionaireMarketingMiracles.com

**Debbie Allen**, '*The Millionaire Entrepreneur Business Builder*', has built and sold numerous million-dollar companies in diverse industries. She has been a successful entrepreneur since the young age of 19, never having had to apply for a job in her life. For the past 15 years, Debbie has presented before thousands of people in over 20 countries around the globe.

She is one of less than 5% of professional women speakers worldwide to have achieved the honor of CSP (Certified Speaking Professional) by both the National Speakers Association and International Speakers Federation. Debbie is also an international marketing mentor and business builder with clients all over the world. She is a bestselling author of five books on business and personal development including her best sellers, *Confessions of Shameless Self-Promoters* and *Skyrocketing Sales*. She has been honored by the U.S. Chamber of Commerce with the prestigious Blue Chip Enterprise Award for overcoming business obstacles and achieving fast business growth. Her expertise has been featured in dozens of publications including, *Entrepreneur, Selling Power* and *Sales & Marketing Excellence.* She is also a regularly featured columnist in *Personal Branding Magazine* and has been featured in four motivational movies including *The Opus* and *The Compass*. Learn more about Debbie at www.DebbieAllen.com.

**Paul** "Turbo Coach" **Avins** is the Author of *Business SOS* and founder of The Business Wealth Club Franchise, whose impressive track record includes starting, growing and selling a number of his own businesses, as well as generating over £100 million in new sales and profits for the businesses he's coached. His unique mix of Business Strategy, Personal Growth, Practical takeaway ideas and infectious energy has inspired

audiences the world over and made him a sought after business growth consultant and key-note speaker. In the last 7 years alone, Paul has personally coached and worked with hundreds of businesses across 79 different industries from start-ups to some of the UK's top companies including VW, Porsche and Salon Success as well as presenting his business growth strategies on stage with other business gurus such Michael Gerber, James Caan and David Gold. His first book, *Business SOS,* is receiving rave reviews and helping business owners make money in today's fast moving and demanding market, and his second book, *Turbo Profits,* is due out in early 2011. Following his own rather late diagnosis of dyslexia, Paul is now dedicated to bringing this issue into the public's consciousness, and he firmly believes that too many of our business stars of the future are misunderstood and incorrectly labeled as failures.
www.Paul-Avins.com  www.TheBusinessWealthClub.com

**Janet Beckers** is the founder of Wonderful Web Group & Niche Partners Pty Ltd. When Janet launched Wonderful Web Women, she had no list, no-one had heard of her and she was down to her last dollar. Within eight weeks of convincing the world's most successful women to support her launch, she had matched her previous 12 months' income, built a list of thousands and won an award for the best membership site on the Internet. Janet is now the founder of a successful and dynamic online community; an international speaker; best-selling author and mentor, and has helped and inspired thousands to create their own success online. She is a multi-award winner, including most recently, Australian Marketer of The Year.
www.WonderfulWebWomen.com

**Gurbaksh Chahal** ('G') was born in India and moved to America aged four, when his parents received a visa for America through a lottery based system in India. His parents had arrived with only $25 to their name, and they struggled at menial jobs to make a future for their four children. For the Chahal family, as for many immigrants, education was paramount, but G left high school at the age of 16 to form Click Agents, an Internet advertising company, which he sold two years later for $40 million. In 2004, he launched a second company, BlueLithium – the next generation in Internet advertising. BlueLithium was named one of the top 100 private companies in America three years in a row by AlwaysOn, and in 2006, it received the highest honor as Top Innovator of the Year. In 2007, G sold BlueLithium to Yahoo®! G is living proof that no matter how humble one's beginnings, there is truly no limit to what an individual can achieve. After he completed his role at Yahoo®!, G signed up with the William Morris Agency. G started on FOX's prime-time network show *The Secret Millionaire*. He has appeared on *The Oprah Winfrey Show, Bonnie Hunt, EXTRA,* and *Neil Cavuto,* among others, and has been profiled in such publications as *The New York Times, Entrepreneur magazine, BusinessWeek, Wall Street Journal, Fortune* and *The San Francisco Chronicle*. He completed his memoir, '*The Dream*', which was globally released in 2008 and now has become required reading in various colleges nationwide. In 2009, he was featured on *Extra TV* as America's Most Eligible Bachelor. Also in 2009, Chahal started his third Company, gWallet, a virtual currency platform for social media. In 2010, Chahal was awarded the Leaders in Management Award and an Honorary Doctorate degree in Commercial Science from Pace University for his career achievements as an entrepreneur. www.Chahal.com

**Dr William Davey** LVO MD LRCP FFHOM AKC, took early retirement in 2001 from his appointment as Physician to Her Majesty the Queen, and was honored by Queen Elizabeth II with the award of Lieutenant of the Royal Victorian Order. Whilst practicing as a General Physician in his London practice, first in Harley Street then at Upper Wimpole Street, Dr Davey pursued his interests in research. These involved not only orthodox medicine, but also in the wider field of complementary medicine. His extensive range of research activities has involved investigating the effects of electroacupunture stimulation of the human central nervous system and the generation of neurochemicals for pain relief, and also the investigation of antibiotic effects of botanical extracts. This resulted in the discovery of a new anti-MRSA and anti Tuberculosis chemical, naturally found in Bee Propolis. This investigation he did as Blackie Research Fellow at the National Heart and Lung Institute in London. This culminated in the award of an MD from Imperial College, London, using the above

discovery. Further investigations of its application in the treatment of leprosy were pursued as Visiting Research Scholar at Green College Oxford, and, as Honorary Medical Director of the Blackie Memorial Foundation, Dr Davey sought to elucidate the efficacy and mode of action of homoeopathy. As a result of his activities, he published papers suggesting ways of overcoming the difficulties of research on homoeopathy and the Standardization of homoeopathic remedies. He was instrumental in establishing the first Chair of Complementary Medicine at the Peninsular University at Exeter. Dr Davey is a Freeman of the City of London and a Liveryman of the Worshipful Company of Barber Surgeons.
www.GeneLifestyle.com

**Gill Fielding** is an international public speaker, a writer and a presenter. She was born into a poor family in the East End of London but, despite humble beginnings, Gill is now a self-made multi-millionaire. Gill realized that she was 'financially free' in 1997 and since then, has worked to share her knowledge with others by facilitating wealth creation through her writing and public speaking. Gill's media CV is extensive and she has been '*Secret Millionaire*' on Channel 4, a business expert on *The Apprentice – You're Fired* show, and a financial commentator for the BBC, ITV and CNBC, as well as appearing in a variety of other TV shows around the world. Gill is currently a financial expert for the BBC and hosts a monthly phone-in for BBC radio, and contributed to ITN and Channel 4's 2010 election coverage. As well as the TV, radio and public media, Gill is a prolific public speaker and has spoken on all five continents on macro economic affairs, wealth creation, financial education, and investing skills, as well as on more personal motivational and inspirational topics. Gill's book, CD, and DVD, *Riches, the Seven Secrets of Wealth You Were Never Told*, were published in January 2010, and is available on Amazon. www.RichesTheMovie.com

**Toby Garbett** is an Olympian and two-time World Champion rower. His unique approach to fitness and well-being was developed through his own experiences as an Olympic athlete. Toby is a highly experienced fitness consultant and Pilates instructor, providing leading-edge fitness training to corporate and private clients. He first represented Great Britain in 1997 aged 19 and went on to compete in five World Championships and attend two Olympic Games. During his long international rowing career, he experienced illness, injury and disappointment, which tested his motivation to the fullest. Bouncing back from these setbacks gave him renewed energy and determination, which he now brings into his work as a personal trainer. As an Olympian, he had access to some of the world's leading coaches, physiotherapists, nutritionists and sport psychologists; and has accumulated a wealth of knowledge and understanding about what it takes to succeed. He brings his in-depth understanding of focus, motivation and self-belief into his work with clients. He works with a range of celebrity clients, youngsters and athletes. Toby is a certified Pilates specialist, teaching good posture and body awareness through his FIT4BUSINESS initiative taking this to the corporate world. www.TobyGarbett.com

 **Mindy Gibbins-Klein** is an international speaker and author and is founder and director of REAL Thought Leaders, The Book Midwife® and Ecademy Press business publishing. She is a highly sought after speaker to executive audiences; she also develops and presents workshops and training programs for top business leaders. She has spoken to thousands of entrepreneurs and executives in twelve countries. In addition to speaking, Mindy also maintains a small list of private consultancy clients who use her services to develop their writing, publishing and speaking strategy, and to plan, write and publish specific books and articles that raise their profiles as REAL thought leaders in the market. Mindy has an MBA in International Business and has taught the post-graduate diploma course for the Chartered Institute of Marketing in the UK. She has an enviable list of over 300 published clients, many of whom have received excellent media coverage and book sales. Mindy has written and been interviewed for articles, radio and television over 100 times on the subject of building a profile as a REAL thought leader, writing, publishing and speaking. She is also a regular columnist for several magazines and online publications, as well as being an expert consultant for three online business communities. She is the author and co-author of four books, several of which have reached the top ten in Business Books on Amazon. www.BookMidwife.com www.Ecademy-Press.com

**Kevin Green** is Wales's most successful residential landlord and property development trainer, owning 267 properties throughout Wales, worth £29 million. He started work as a dairy farmer on his family's farm and built up the family business during the process of renewal and grief after losing his sister Julie to Lupus aged 20. Since then, Kevin has vowed never to waste time. In 2001, via a scholarship entitled *Mindset for Success - studying the attitudes and personalities of high achievers*, Kevin started a quest for knowledge of success by interviewing top entrepreneurs globally. One of the themes that stood out was that some of the most successful people in the world would often make decisions more from the heart than from the head. Over the next eight years, Kevin built up his large property portfolio, and in 2010, he established his own training company Kevin Green Wealth Training. Kevin is also linked closely with Make-A-Wish Foundation® UK. RDF and Channel 4's decision to include Kevin in *The Secret Millionaire* series in 2009 has been a life-altering experience for him, consolidating many of his fears and belief systems. Support for the wonderful causes Kevin has chosen to support during filming will be ongoing, building relationships for the future. www.KevinGreen.co.uk www.PropertyTrain.biz

**Amanda van der Gulik**, a homeschooling mom-preneur, is passionate about empowering kids with life-skills, self-esteem building skills, and most especially, about teaching children and teens about money. Amanda also likes to decorate cakes in her spare time, while travelling the globe with her young family. You can find out more about Amanda and how she empowers kids and cake decorators on her various websites at: www.TeachingChildrenAboutMoney.com; www.AllowanceSecrets.com; www.GetUnstuckForKids.com; www.FunCakeDecoratingIdeas.com

**Stephanie J Hale** is a publishing expert and writing coach... helping authors to write, promote and pitch their books. She is author of *Millionaire Women, Millionaire You*, which features powerful money-making strategies from 12 women who rose from zero to millionaire. She is co-founder of The Millionaire

Bootcamp for Women and founder of Oxford Literary Consultancy. Get your FREE sample chapter containing proven wealth tips at:
www.MillionaireWomenMillionaireYou.com/free
www.MillionaireWomenResources.com

**Andy Harrington** is one of the world's premier authorities on the psychology of peak performance, personal achievement and the art of influence. He has inspired hundreds of thousands of people across the world to achieve their goals and transform the quality of their lives. Andy is also sought after by Hollywood movie stars, talented entrepreneurs, and some of the world's best-loved speakers when they need to land that big contract or sell to the masses for huge paydays. A successful entrepreneur, Andy Harrington has built several multi-million pound companies. His first company has now pulled in over £46 million. He is a world-class speaker having spoken at some of the most prestigious venues including recently at the London O2 Arena to more than 6,500 people. Andy is best-loved for his ability to inspire an audience to action through his own special brand of motivation. He uniquely combines a deep understanding of human psychology with the mind management tools that can get even the most disheartened to overcome their own self-imposed limitation to success.
www.powertoachieve.co.uk/freedvd

**Emma Harrison** is a respected Entrepreneur and the Chairman, owner and founder of A4e. A4e is the Global leader in Social and Welfare reform and employs 4,000 staff across 250 centers worldwide — working on the front line of public services. It is the principal supplier and Prime Contractor to The UK Government's services such as the Flexible New Deal, Legal Aid Helpline, Social Care, Education for Offenders, Business Enterprise, Youth Vocational centers and much more. A4e is renowned for developing and delivering social change on behalf of Governments. Its stated mission and Emma's driving passion is to 'Improve people's lives'. Emma has been awarded and recognized as one of the UK's leading entrepreneurs, e.g. First Women Award for Public Service 2010, Nat West Everywoman, Front Cover of Director Magazine IoD, Veuve Clicquot Woman of the Year Finalist, Top Women Entrepreneur

**Dr Jane Lewis** is a UK-based coach, consultant and trainer. She specializes in offering tailored career coaching programs to women who have hit the glass ceiling at work, and to entrepreneurs who are new to using the Internet in their business. She has enjoyed a varied international career, working for large global enterprises such as Exxon/Esso as well as small organizations. She has had her own coaching business since 1998. Jane is also a student and teacher of Hawaiian Huna, and holds a PhD in Esoteric Studies – looking at practical spirituality for modern leaders. When she's not coaching or consulting, she plays the cello in an Irish pub band and goes to Hawaii twice a year. www.TheCareerSuccessDoctor.com

**Caroline Marsh** is a highly successful buy-to-let property investor, who appeared in Channel 4's (C4) *The Secret Millionaire*. Thanks to the highly cash-positive portfolio she had built, together with her natural determination, resilience, generosity, capability and integrity, she was able to make a real difference to two projects in Toxteth, Liverpool. The Dingle Community Learning project – which provides computers and other learning facilities for young adults in Toxteth - has had their roof fixed and premises refurbished, and Dijuana, a single mother who offers after-school activities to keep young people off the streets, has had both financial assistance and personal and business development mentoring from Caroline. Since she filmed for C4, she has been working locally with the Mayor of Swindon, her MP and local businesses, to make a difference, encouraging businesses to sponsor and support young people in enterprise projects. In early 2009, she helped launch the *Make Your Mark With A Tenner* campaign in Swindon – a nationwide initiative, headed by Dragons' Den star Peter Jones, where schoolchildren are given ten pounds and a month to come up with a small business that contributes to the local community and also makes a profit. Caroline got both major employers and small businesses together to commit to share their expertise with the schools. Caroline was on the judging panel for *Enterprising Britain 2009*, to find the most enterprising place in the UK; has been working alongside Esther Rantzen as part of the Family Commission with the *4 Children* charity, and was also on the judging panel for *Women On Their Way, 2010*. Since the C4 programme aired, Caroline has become well-respected as an inspirational and motivational speaker, and she travels around the country talking to groups of women in business and entrepreneurial young people. She has also set up a personal and business development coaching business with a partner, Millionaire Mindset mentor, Jan Alam. Their *Secrets of Success Group* is committed to sharing success fundamentals and helping people reprogram themselves to achieve their goals. www.CarolineMarsh.com

**Curly Martin** An international speaker, founder of Achievement Specialists, author of The Coaching Handbook series, expert on Britain's Next Top Coach, Fellow member and International Head of Ethics and Standards with the International Coaching Institute. www.AchievementSpecialists.co.uk

**Katie Moore** is an entrepreneur investor. With 30 years of business experience in this field, she combines her natural ability to listen and take action to find solutions to business problems. She enjoys facing the challenges that today's difficult business environment throws at us. Current projects include building solar PV farms in the UK along with an online community who can share in the profits from the farms. The youngest of six children, Katie was brought up on a small-holding in Somerset; educated at a convent and attended college, qualifying with the Institute of Training & Development, and then with the Institute of Personnel & Management. Katie is owner, partner and shareholder in six businesses over 30 years ranging from renewable energy, affiliate marketing, leisure, health and an online business community. When asked to define 'success', she says: "*I think success is synonymous with happiness rather than with affluence. It's only when you find satisfaction with what you're doing that you are really successful.*" Katie believes her greatest achievement is building an online community of 70,000 entrepreneurs. Her biggest obstacle to date has been in being a single parent trying to be successful in a predominantly male-orientated business society - overcome purely by sheer hard work and determination. Katie is inspired by people who help others and still manage to make money! www.KatieMoore.co.uk www.BusinessEssentialsAcademy.com

**Kelly Morrisey** has created a connection with people from around the world with her creation of www.ABetterLifeAfterDivorce.com. Kelly provides international divorce recovery and personal growth strategies, tools and resources, and has uplifted and enlightened many of those experiencing the trauma and crisis of divorce. People from all over the world schedule private tele-sessions with Kelly Morrisey and seek her counsel. She holds tele-seminars revolving around the areas of divorce recovery, personal growth and building a strong, loving relationship. Kelly is respected and endorsed by many of the top experts in the personal development and relationship field and is the author of *A Better Life After Divorce*. She is also a Divorce Recovery Workshop counselor and writer of *Finding Love After Divorce, Igniting Your Life's Passion After Divorce,* and *What Do Divorced Men and Women REALLY Want?* Kelly assists you in focusing on what was positive in your past and what you need to do to succeed in your new life with your new freedom and develop your personal power to live the life that you've always imagined.
www.ABetterLifeAfterDivorce.com  www.ANewYouAfterDivorce.com

**Marie O'Riordan** has been working on the air in Radio, TV and and has been an award-winning short filmmaker since she was just 13 years old. Quantum leaps in her career have seen her report as a Journalist for CNN aged just 20. The late Nobel Peace Prize winner, Mother Teresa, gave Marie the last interview she ever gave in her home in Calcutta, India, before her death in 1997. Marie was then aged just 22. This profound experience helped to change the course of the rest of Marie's life by leading her to want to reach out and touch the lives of billions of people around the world through her many amazing gifts in the communications arena. Marie O'Riordan has been interviewing Hollywood's elite and scores of Academy Award winners face-to-face for many years such as Paul Newman, Michael Caine, Quentin Tarantino, Charlize Theron, Cate Blanchett, Renee Zellweger and many, many more. Marie is also an Enlightened Philanthropist who volunteers and makes hard-hitting documentaries in the Third World. She first volunteered abroad aged just 16.
www.MarieORiordanInternational.com

**Penny Power** is a Social Networking Expert, Author, Entrepreneur and founder of Ecademy. She is a published author, a highly engaging speaker and one of the UK's most inspirational and successful female entrepreneurs. In 1998, Penny founded Ecademy, the UK's first social network for business, with her husband, Thomas. Ecademy is now a global operation with members in over 200 countries. Underpinning the network's success is the powerful feeling of being part of a community and the strong intention that each member has towards supporting one another. Penny's unique contribution to the world of social networking is that she has created a hugely successful network herself. She is the public face and voice of online networking. Penny is a strategic adviser to the National Consortium of University Entrepreneurs (NACUE). In 2010, Penny was invited to join James Caan's EBA Millionaire Mentor team. Penny is also no stranger to the media spotlight. She is a regular contributor and commentator on Social Networking and business, is a columnist for the *Daily Express* and regularly speaks at conferences and events across the globe. Her latest book, *Know Me, Like Me, Follow Me* (August 2009) is an exceptional help to anyone wanting to learn how to future-proof themselves and their businesses. www.Ecademy.com

**John Purkiss** recruits senior executives and board members for a wide range of companies. In his spare time he takes photographs and invests in high-growth businesses. John is the co-author of *How to be Headhunted*; *Ken Purkiss - 50 Photos*; and *Brand You*. Further information can be found at www.JohnPurkiss.com

**Kathleen Ronald**, "Queen of Business Networking," is an unparalleled networker, an internationally renowned speaker, trainer, business consultant and the founder of Speaktacular. Kathleen has more than 27 years of experience providing custom, inspirational keynotes, training seminars and consultancy to Fortune 500 companies, small business and professional associations. Kathleen excels at helping people shed the cookie-cutter approach to prospecting and develop personal, authentic strategies that 'build their net worth by building their network.' She is known for helping people leverage 10 hours of networking to turn into tens of thousands worth of business! With a lifelong reputation for uniting people and building communities, she has founded successful networking groups, Fortune 10/10 (a women's investment group), and WOW (Women of Wealth) Ventures and co-founded WIN (Women in Networking). As a highly sought-after business consultant, her clients experience first-year revenue increases of 20 to 50%. Kathleen was awarded the Top Business Consultant for San Jose, CA in 2009 – 2010. She is also featured in several books, *Miracle Thinking* by Randy Peyser, and *Got Experts* by Michele Moliter.

 **Seema Sharma**'s privileged upbringing was a far cry from the slums of Dharavi, the largest slum in southeast Asia in her country of origin, India, where she lived for 2 weeks in search of local charities to support, during the making of *Slumdog Secret Millionaire*. Seema was born in July 1967 in Lusaka, Zambia (Central Africa), to parents of Indian descent who had been born and brought up in Kenya. She is a third generation British Indian – her grandparents left the village of Ropar in the Punjab on a Dhow boat, in search of a better life in Africa, despite the fact that her great grandfather was a village clerk in a highly respected civil service post. She was brought up with an awareness of her cultural background, but concedes that although some of the traditions passed down by migrant generations are colonial or even archaic in modern India, they provide Indians abroad, especially those from previous generations, with security and a sense of identity. Educated at the International School of Lusaka (ISL) in Zambia until 'O' Level, then at Roedean School for Girls in Brighton for her 'A' Levels, Seema went on to study Dentistry at Guy's Hospital in the 80s and won several awards in the 90s for the rapid growth of her dental practice in Docklands, citing receiving a business award from Richard Branson at the age of 28 as one of her most memorable career moments. She was featured in the Asian Women of Achievements book in 1995 and more recently went on to be featured in the list of the top 50 most influential dentists published by a leading trade journal, *Dentistry*. www.TheSharmaFoundation.org www.dentabyte.co.uk  www.medibyte.com www.SmileImpressions.com

**Peter Thomson** is regarded as one of the UK's leading strategists on business and personal growth. Starting in business in 1972, he built three successful companies – selling the last to a public company, after only five years trading, for £4.2M, enabling him to retire at the age of 42. Since that time, Peter has concentrated on sharing his proven methods for business and personal success via audio and video programs, books, seminars and conference speeches. With over 100 audio and 100 video programs, three books and numerous booklets and guides written and recorded, he is Nightingale Conant's leading UK author. Peter's widely acclaimed monthly audio newsletter, *The Achievers Edge*, now in its 13th year of publication, has sold over 250,000 copies around the globe. As editor of *tgiMondays*, Peter provides a free weekly Motivation Monday Message to over 23,000 success-minded people worldwide. In 1999, the American Intercontinental University in London – with permission granted by the American Government - awarded Peter an Honorary Doctorate (Doctor of Letters) for his work in communication skills and helping others to succeed in life. www.PeterThomson.com

**Emma Tiebens** is the Founder of The Relational Marketer. She is passionate about teaching entrepreneurs how to create a powerful online presence for their business using technology to build and foster business relationships with people they wouldn't have been able to reach before. As a result of that relationship, they feel the need to invest in whatever it is that you offer - product, system or service. As a Mentor, Consultant and Coach, she teaches entrepreneurs to create an 'Authentic' brand online that will enable them to be trusted to gain more loyal customers, raving fans and potential Joint Venture partnerships. She shows entrepreneurs how to leverage social media, video marketing and technology to reach a greater audience. As a speaker, she speaks about the importance of 'Relationships First' and she teaches entrepreneurs a step by step process of Attracting, Nurturing and Retaining your perfect clients online and offline! As an Author, she has written a book - *Attracting Customers For Life* and has co-authored a book with Mari Smith and 19 other authors worldwide called *The Relationship Age*. www.TheRelationshipMarketer.com

# Share With Us

We would love to hear about your reaction to the life lessons in this book and also to hear about YOUR life lessons.

- How did the life lessons in this book impact your life?

- What insights did you gain?

- What actions were you inspired to take?

- What results did you have?

Come and share your reactions and results and your own life lessons in our community at www.UltimateLifeLessonsClub.com. They could be included in future books we are planning in this series.

We hope you enjoy reading this book and expanding on your learning from doing the exercises.

Have a fabulous life!